UNLOCKING DOORS TO SELF-ESTEEM

C. Lynn Fox, Ph.D.
and
Francine Lavin Weaver, M.A.

Foreword by Dr. Shirley E. Forbing

Jalmar Press
Rolling Hills Estates, California 90274

ISBN: 0-915190-60-5

Library of Congress Catalog Number: 89-084064

Printed in the United States of America

Printing No.: 10 9 8 7 6 5 4 3 2 1

DEDICATION

This book is dedicated to our families:

Ruth	Joseph
Ava	Florence
Chuck	Butch
Don	Cynthia
Dean	Janet

. . .who have always made us feel like WINNERS.

ACKNOWLEDGEMENTS

Unlocking Doors to Self-Esteem is now a reality! We would like to thank the following people for their guidance and encouragement throughout the planning, development, and completion of our book:

- Brad Winch for his encouragement and support in helping us to make it all happen.

- Joanne LaMonte and Janet Lovelady, editors for B.L. Winch & Associates who helped us finalize and polish our book.

- Mary Button and Janet Lovelady for coordinating our book's production.

- Natalie Antes for typing the manuscript and being very patient with our demands. We think you are great!

- Jane Brucker for artistic conceptualization.

- Jo Bain
- Larry Hart
- Ellen Kagan
- Jerry Norman
- Pete Pitard
- Dan Rock
- Becky Vroom

- Michael Fares
- Gregory Hayes
- Margaret Layne
- Janis Oetgen
- Dale Ranson
- Neil Rothschild
- Shelley Weitzberg

- Nancy Hanna
- Wally Hirsh
- Dave Murray
- Meg Peckham
- Azneef Roberts
- Haze Rufo

for fieldtesting and/or reviewing our lessons. Their efforts and feedback will be more than appreciated by the educators who use this book.

- Margaret Layne
- Meg Peckham
- Betsy Pray

and their students for contributing original prose and poetry to add extra meaning to our book.

- Barbara Begg
- Gordon Settle
- Wendy Dallas
- Shelley Weitzberg
- Brad Sales
- Andrea Wieder

for helping with the editing. Their aid and moral support helped to lighten our load.

- Shirley Andrews and Donna Taylor for compiling the Annotated Bibliography of Young Adult Fiction appearing in Chapter VII.

There have been numerous others — both family and friends — who have encouraged us to finish this two-year endeavor.

THANKS TO ALL OF YOU!!! You assisted us in making *Unlocking Doors to Self-Esteem* a reality.

CONTENTS

Chapter VII. Finding New Doors: Other Resources

FOREWORD

In my position as a professor of preservice and inservice teachers at San Diego State University, San Diego, California, I have depended upon material in the book, *Unlocking Doors to Self-Esteem*, by Fox and Weaver, to add a necessary dimension to my courses. *Unlocking Doors* has a sound research base with adolescents. The activities within it reflect the special needs of this turbulent stage.

University professors need to model good teaching techniques for teachers in training. *Unlocking Doors* provides for that and also allows for the practical application of theory to reinforce learning. Student teachers and credentialed teachers alike have used lessons from this book with adolescents and were uniformly enthusiastic!! Feedback from them revealed that the activities from *Unlocking Doors* enabled them to understand their students in a way not possible with traditional assignments. They also reported a bonding phenomena of the class as a whole over the semester with the continued use of *Unlocking Doors* lessons. For those youth who are generally "left out," who are alienated, such bonding experiences are crucial. From a practical view, teachers found that they could infuse the *Unlocking Doors* activities into the regular curriculum. With an already overcrowded curriculum, this efficiency is beneficial. Moreover, most of the lessons are designed to fit into the 55 minute class periods.

With the identification of drug abuse as the No. 1 problem facing schools (Gallup Poll, 1985-1988), it becomes imperative that we give a higher priority than we have in the past to that aspect of the curriculum which deals with self-esteem, the feelings of belonging, values clarification, problem solving and interpersonal communication. Deficits in these areas have been identified for youth at risk for drug abuse. *Unlocking Doors* offers realistic and easy to implement lessons in these areas.

Dr. Shirley E. Forbing
College of Education
San Diego State University
Co-author, *Fighting Substance Abuse in Schools and Communities*

TRAININGS IN CLASSROOM MANAGEMENT
AND BUILDING SELF-ESTEEM
offered by Dr. C. Lynn Fox

Dr. Fox offers a wide variety of inservice presentations; many are supplemented with books she has written. Programs include keynote addresses, seminars, workshops and long-term comprehensive programs designed to meet specific needs, goals and objectives; all are focused on improving classroom skills.

- **Social Acceptance: Key to Mainstreaming.** This workshop and book are for teachers concerned with the social and emotional development of their students in the classroom. Areas emphasized are how to help teachers become good role models, how to promote students' self-concept and perception of others and activities to promote social acceptance.

- **Communicating to Make Friends.** A step-by-step program for the elementary classroom teacher who wants to help change the attitudes of the "established" student toward the "isolated" child. Areas covered in the workshop and book are how to develop social skills through academic channels such as oral and written communication, techniques for assessment, ideas for weekly art lessons and how to change the social climate in the classroom with fun and easy activities.

- **Unlocking Doors to Self-Esteem.** This workshop and book present many innovative ideas and suggestions to make the secondary classroom a more positive learning experience — socially, emotionally and academically — for students and teachers. Activities included help eliminate stereotypical and social barriers, enhance self-concept and develop effective communication skills.

- **Improving Classroom Behavior and Management.** This workshop will show how to set up an effective, well-organized classroom which prevents behavioral problems. Other topics include reasons why students misbehave, the differences between consequences and punishment, the development and implementation of group and individual management programs and better reward systems.

- **Substance Abuse.** Dr. Fox gives an overview in this workshop of the problems and contributing factors. She explains what can be done to attack the drug epidemic in the home, school and community. Also presented are ways to identify children who are abusing, what enabling means and resources available in the fight.

- **Effective Mainstreaming Strategies.** This workshop provides helping professionals with educational and social strategies plus practical and fun activities to mainstream special students into the classroom. Other areas covered are how to match teaching methods to learning needs, how to take the mystery out of special education and how to build social acceptance for all students and reduce social tension.

- **Working with Chapter 1 and Migrant Education Students.** Workshops available are "Teacher Expectations and Their Effects on Student Performance" and "IEP Development and Maintenance."

To contact Dr. Fox, call or write:
128 Sugar Loaf Drive
Tiburon, California 94920
(415) 435-9248

OPENING THE DOOR:

INTRODUCTION

CHAPTER I

 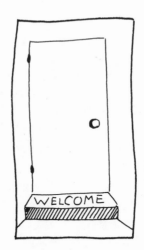 

OPENING THE DOOR: INTRODUCTION

Chapter I

Anyone having had minimal contact with adolescents will agree that this developmental stage is one of constant challenges and confusion. Secondary school students, ages 12 through 17, are caught between the security of childhood and the privileges, enjoyment, and responsibilities of adulthood. An identity crisis occurs and continues throughout this age. Adolescents are constantly exploring and struggling with their self-awareness and self-confidence. During this time, their bodies are physically changing, which also affects their self-concepts. As a result of this turmoil, many adolescents do not feel good about

UNLOCKING DOORS TO SELF-ESTEEM

I was walking down a dark and misty corridor
when I came to a dead end at a door.
I had nowhere to go but through the door.
But who knows what awaits me on the other side?
I opened the door a crack and saw a light.
A glimmering, shining light, full of hope.
I opened the door wider and felt a warmth.
A glowing, comfortable warmth, full of love.
I opened the door all the way,
and I found you — my friend.

By Julie Peckham
San Diego, CA

themselves. Moreover, they are trying to identify their social status among their peers and gain independence. They are constantly experimenting with different social roles in search of appropriate means of interaction and communication.

Although adolescents experience these challenges, the majority of them live through puberty with little emotional damage. However, too many have a difficult time adjusting to these social and physiological changes. For some, the end results are social isolation and rejection which can be devastating to their self-esteem.

Society places additional expectations on the secondary student which add to the trauma of adolescence. To begin with, secondary students now graduating from high school must prove competence in the basic academic areas and are tested to verify their knowledge. Their diplomas are tailored to speak affirmatively to the community about their readiness to survive in society. This survival not only requires academic ability but demands appropriate social expertise, especially communication skills.

Further demands are made on secondary students to obtain skills to secure and maintain a job. Although these expectations and their accompanying pressures exist, little training is provided to assist students in meeting them.

Given the adolescents' needs and society's expectations for secondary students, teachers are put in a difficult position further complicating the situation. Under the current school structure, secondary teachers see 150 to 180 students per day. Their teacher training emphasized the academic curriculum, particularly their chosen subject areas, yet they are now being asked, with no additional training, to meet their students' social needs.

To add to this dilemma, secondary teachers are confronted with students from diverse backgrounds. In every classroom, there are usually two or three students who for a variety of reasons are not accepted by their classmates. A class may be comprised of students from many cultures, areas of the country, and/or races. However unfortunate, the reality is that stereotypic barriers often put a strain on the interaction of diversified groups within these populations. Usually students who are in a minority in a given situation are the ones who feel socially rejected.

HAIKU

Feeling frustrated
Trying to make the difference
Winning the battle.

By Julia Moser, San Diego, CA

Many teachers have students from special education classes who have been placed in their rooms on a part or full-time basis. This population of students brings extra problems. Often their self-confidence is deflated and because of this they assume one of two roles: 1) withdrawing from their peers, or 2) acting out to receive peer attention. Both responses tend to antagonize peers and result in various forms of social isolation. Many of these students, such as the learning disabled, not only have poor self-concepts but also lack adequate social skills. They are in double jeopardy.

To complete the cycle, the peer group perceives this population as different and therefore does not accept or include these students within their circle of friends. This is also true of the "hidden handicapped" such as students with moderate learning disabilities and mild mental retardation.

Other students who may have problems in their peer relationships are those who are overweight or physically unattractive; gifted students with poor social skills; and students who join the class after the beginning of the school year. All of these students bring with them their own particular needs.

Overweight or physically unattractive students go through extremely difficult ordeals relating to their peers. Particularly, at this age and social level when physical appearance is a primary concern, they are placed at a definite disadvantage socially.

For many highly intelligent students, it is difficult to interact comfortably with their classmates. Thus they avoid situations where they could learn important social skills. Yet, whether or not they have these skills, there are times when they will be forced to relate on a personal level. When required to do so, they seem to "turn the tables" and try to intimidate their classmates with their intellectual ability. This action causes more rejection and further denies the individuals involved an important learning experience.

I USED TO HAVE A FRIEND — A POEM

Farther we drift, not accepting each other at all
We used to be "buddies" — a pair — one of a kind
Now she walks away with the new girl.

By Julia Moser, San Diego, CA

Last, but not least, are students who join the class at various times throughout the year. It is difficult for these students to integrate because the class has developed a social structure prior to their arrival. The class has already had the opportunity to share many common experiences that the new student has missed.

This potpourri of students presents a constant struggle for acceptance of selves and others by each classmate. Stereotypic barriers keep students from getting to know and reaching out to each other in a climate of positive support and understanding.

The group dynamics in each class that the secondary teacher confronts every day cannot be ignored. Little of the valuable academic information will be processed unless students learn to accept themselves and their peers. *Unlocking Doors to Self-Esteem* was conceived to address these needs and to provide concrete activities that teachers can implement at the secondary level.

Beneficiaries

The activities and suggestions in *Unlocking Doors to Self-Esteem* are geared toward students and teachers at the junior and senior high school level. Specifically, teachers in the six different subject areas of English, drama and communications, social science, science, career education, and physical education will find these interesting. Teachers of bilingual, multi-cultural, gifted, and special education classes will discover that the activities address the special social needs of their students and are beneficial and motivational to *all* students. Career and vocational education teachers and counselors will profit by infusing the social and academic curricula. Our intention in seeking widespread adoption of this philosophy of learning is to enable many secondary teachers and students to upgrade the quality of their learning environment.

Although all students will gain from involvement in the program, these activities will further enhance the social development and acceptance of students who are:

- mainstreamed
- gifted with poor social skills
- obese or physically unattractive
- racially different
- culturally different
- withdrawn
- acting out/aggressive
- new student in class

Considerations

Unlocking Doors to Self-Esteem was developed with the secondary teacher in mind! In its development, we took many factors into consideration, including the reality that most secondary teachers have had limited training in how to teach or handle the social needs of their students. Chapter II gives a detailed explanation of why there is a need for teachers to acquaint themselves with, obtain, and utilize activities that relate to the social and interpersonal needs of their students. Instructional methods and specific lesson plans for providing necessary training to adolescents in these areas are central themes of *Unlocking Doors to Self-Esteem*. These methods and lesson plans are clear, concise, and can be implemented without any extra training.

We also recognize that secondary education is focused primarily on teaching the academics, especially the designated subject areas such as English, science, and social science. We concentrated our efforts and skills to avoid interfering with this goal. Our philosophy is that the social curriculum should be "part of" or

THINGS WE DO

Giggling, teasing, telephone, noise,
Talking, dreaming, babysitting, and boys;
Slumber parties, secrets, it must be a true love.
12:00 a.m. rap sessions, junk food,
and sharing what we dream of.
Dieting, stereos, concerts, tests, homework,
cheerleading, giving it all your absolute best.
Shopping, movies with your best friend,
hoping your teens will never end.

By Julie Peckham
San Diego, CA

infused into the existing academic curriculum rather than taught as a separate unit of study. To separate these two curricula for secondary teachers and students would be impractical as well as ineffective. Specifically, we created activities and lesson plans utilizing the required content objectives relative to the specific subject areas. Yet these activities have a special twist to them; they bring in social skills training in a natural and meaningful manner. The activities also add excitement and motivation to the subject area. In turn, these aspects reinforce and enrich the ordinary learning process. Students learn the necessary concepts with less energy and with less resistance — elements that make both learning and teaching more enjoyable.

Another aspect considered throughout the planning of this book is the time constraint at the secondary level. Teachers usually have 45-55 minutes per day with their students. Thus, all activities are designed to fit within this time frame.

A final factor we considered was the lack of sufficient funding to implement new programs. *Unlocking Doors to Self-Esteem* requires few, if any, extra materials or resources that are not readily available. Creativity and imagination are the only extra tools required to enrich the units or lessons suggested.

Goals and Objectives

There are three major social goals of *Unlocking Doors to Self-Esteem*:

GOAL 1. To provide teachers with activities to foster positive self-concepts and self-confidence in *all* students.

GOAL 2. To provide methods, strategies, and activities to assist students in exploring their attitudes, feelings and actions toward others. These activities will help eliminate stereotypical and social barriers such as: sex, race, culture, age, and levels of ability.

GOAL 3. To help teachers facilitate students' positive social interaction skills. The included activities are designed to promote positive relationships with others.

Each activity in *Unlocking Doors to Self-Esteem* will meet at least one of these goals, and some may overlap. To determine which goals are highlighted in the lesson, refer to the chapter numbers. Chapter IV activities deal primarily with Goal 1. Goal 2 is the focus in Chapter V. Goal 3 is stressed in Chapter VI.

Along with addressing the social goals for secondary students, we have attempted to meet the following objectives which are directly related to secondary teachers' needs:

OBJECTIVE 1. To assist secondary teachers in establishing a class in which *all* students are accepted socially by their classmates.

OBJECTIVE 2. To aid secondary teachers in modifying their curriculum to include social concepts related to self-concept development, attitude change, and social interaction.

OBJECTIVE 3. To provide secondary teachers with field-tested activities that combine the development of social skills with the existing academic curriculum.

OBJECTIVE 4. To facilitate secondary teachers in their own self-evaluation.

OBJECTIVE 5. To provide teachers with suggestions for improving their image as role models for their students.

OBJECTIVE 6. To furnish teachers with current research and empirical data relative to secondary students' social skills and attitudes.

OBJECTIVE 7. To give teachers over 100 field tested activities and lessons to incorporate social skills training into their courses.

OBJECTIVE 8. To equip teachers with general ideas and suggestions for improving their classes motivationally, socially, and academically.

OBJECTIVE 9. To present activities to use as an impetus for the creation of new ideas for enhancing the climate of secondary classes.

OBJECTIVE 10. To assist secondary teachers in enjoying their students and their profession more.

Organization

Overview of Chapters. This book includes seven chapters. "Opening the Door," Chapter I, presents the objectives and philosophy behind *Unlocking Doors to Self-Esteem.* "Doors That Have Been Opened," Chapter II, provides the reader with the theoretical concepts as well as empirical data relative to the social development of adolescents. "The Master Key: The Teacher," Chapter III, deals with ways in which teachers can become more effective models for their students. Further, it presents ideas and suggestions to help teachers avoid "burnout" and stress. This chapter emphasizes the importance of the teacher.

Chapters IV, V, and VI are the focal points of our book. These three chapters present the more than 100 field tested lesson plans or units of study that can be implemented into the following six subject areas:

1) English

2) Drama and Communications

3) Social Sciences

4) Science

5) Career Education

6) Physical Education

Each chapter pinpoints one of the major goals of our book. "A Special Door," Chapter IV, is filled with activities that teachers can implement to enhance the self-concept and confidence of their students. "Opening the Door Wider," Chapter V, focuses on lessons designed to encourage students to explore their attitudes, feelings, and actions toward others. These activities motivate students to evaluate stereotypic values and social barriers such as sex, handicaps, culture, religion, race, and age. They will also help students identify their own feelings and develop plans for change.

HAIKU

I'm not accepted
> *Watching from the fringe of things*
>> *See me! I'm alive!*

>>> *By Julia Moser*
>>> *San Diego, CA*

"Keeping the Door Open," Chapter VI, takes the social process a step further and provides teachers with activities, methods, and strategies to enhance their students' positive social interaction skills. Positive and effective peer relationships are a major goal of the methods presented in this chapter.

Unlocking Doors to Self-Esteem ends with "Finding New Doors," Chapter VII. This chapter lists numerous resources relating to social skills training for adolescent junior and/or senior high school students. Also listed are books for students and teachers, films and filmstrips, and various manipulative materials including games and simulation activities.

General Information. There are at least five activities for each subject area that deal with the three goals of our book. Readers can identify the activities designed especially for their area(s) of interest by observing the circled symbols in the upper corner of each lesson.

| English | Drama & Comm. | Social Science | Sciences | Career Education | Physical Education |

Teachers should look through all the activities regardless of the subjects they teach. Many lessons can overlap or be applied to their intended academic area. They may inspire other ideas that can be used to accomplish the same goals.

The poetry and prose included in this book were written by secondary students and have been included for the reader's enjoyment as well as to display products developed by adolescent students given the opportunity. Original poems and prose can provide teachers with insights into what their students may be thinking or feeling. These models may also be shared with students to motivate them to create their own.

Lesson Format. The activities in *Unlocking Doors to Self-Esteem* were field tested by junior and senior high school teachers. They vary in presentation and implementation. They include role-playing, simulations, group discussions, multisensory presentations and responses, group problem solving, classroom games, and the utilization of community resources. We strived to make the activities meaningful, goal-directed, practical, and yet motivating and exciting.

THE FRIEND PIE

2   *Cups of Love*
3/4 *Tablespoon of Kindness*
1/2 *Teaspoon of Sharing*
1/2 *Cup of Learning*
    A tad of ginger
    A bit of spice
    And a big, fat smile will make it nice.

By Tara Nicholson
Oceanside, CA

We hope they will serve as an impetus for teachers to create their own ideas using the philosophy of infusion introduced in *Unlocking Doors to Self-Esteem*.

The lessons also vary in length. Some are geared for 45-55 minute class periods. Others can be expanded into an entire unit of study such as the "Running for You" lesson. Many have been designed to be used as "warm-up" or motivational lessons that will encourage student interest in the academic unit of study to follow. The resume activity entitled "A Picture of the Positive Me" is an example of this motivational, interest-catching technique.

In order to facilitate ease of use, each lesson complies with the following format:

TITLE

Subject: **Grade Level:**

Content Objective: This tells teachers what existing academic objective relates to the particular lesson.

Social Objective: Each social objective agrees with one of the three major goals of this book.

Materials: Materials needed to implement the lesson are listed here. Most are easily accessible in any school setting.

Directions: Specific instructions to teachers are presented here.

Time: These may vary depending on students, teachers, and follow-through or enrichment activities introduced.

Notes to Teacher: Concepts for discussion and suggested enrichment activities appear in this section.

DOORS THAT HAVE BEEN OPENED:

THEORIES & RESEARCH

CHAPTER II

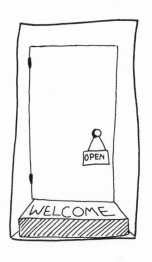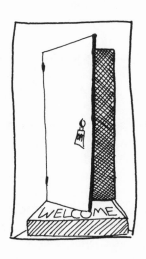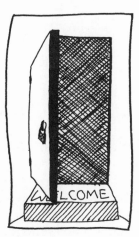

DOORS THAT HAVE BEEN OPENED: THEORY & RESEARCH

Chapter II

When trying to address secondary students' social needs as well as their teachers' concerns about the limits of classroom structure, as authors of *Unlocking Doors to Self-Esteem*, we found a number of questions that needed to be answered:

1. What factors contribute to positive interpersonal relationships?
2. Given the challenges of adolescent social development, what factors contribute to the acceptance and inclusion of self and others?
3. How can stereotypic barriers and prejudices be eliminated?
4. What strategies and techniques can teachers use to facilitate positive social growth in their secondary students?

In an attempt to answer these questions, we went to the library to explore "doors that have been opened." We examined and studied the theories and research available in the areas of attraction, adolescent friendship formation, elimination of stereotypes, and successful learning strategies. We also conducted our own study to identify traits important to adolescents when they select their friends. This study also led to our discovery of the interest areas shared by adolescents. We incorporated this information when developing our innovative curriculum as well as deciding on methods of presenting the lessons. The following sections cover some of the theories and research that provided the foundation for *Unlocking Doors to Self-Esteem*.

Attraction Theories

An in-depth study of the literature revealed four factors that contribute to positive interpersonal relationships and/or friendships. These elements evolved from two theories that explain why people are attracted to one another: the Cognitive Balance Theory (Byrne & Griffitt, 1973) and the Reinforcement

Theory (Byrne, Griffitt & Stefaniak, 1967). For convenience these factors are listed below:

1. **Proximity** — The closer the proximity, the greater the amount of information individuals know about each other. Consequently, this increased frequency of interaction provides them with opportunities to get acquainted and build a positive relationship (Byrne, 1961).
2. **Desire for the esteem of others** — People tend to like those who like them, or who see them in a positive light. This gives testimony to these individuals that they are functioning in a logical and acceptable manner (Byrne, Griffitt, & Stefaniak, 1967).
3. **Similarity of Attitudes** — People seek commonalities of attitudes and personalities. They perceive themselves as being more similar to those they like and also tend to like people with whom they have things in common (Byrne & Griffitt, 1973; Darley & Berscheid, 1967).
4. **Cooperation vs. Competition** — People tend to like others who cooperate with them in their attempts to attain personal goals and rewards. They tend to dislike those who hinder or contradict their quest for self-fulfillment (Berscheid & Walster, 1969).

These four factors were incorporated into *Unlocking Doors to Self-Esteem* in a conscious manner. Considering the importance of proximity, we developed numerous activities promoting opportunities for interaction. Students work in small groups or pairs to accomplish an assigned task, rather than independently or in isolation. To increase involvement opportunities, some lessons suggest homework activities requiring prior communication and planning with classmates. Also, we designed lessons that provide hands-on experiences or field work bringing students closer to real situations that model and reinforce various social concepts.

In an attempt to increase each student's opportunity to experience acceptance and esteem from others, many of the lessons focus on allowing all students to "shine" in front of their peers. Additionally, activities are stressed that encourage students to exchange ideas and feelings so their classmates' previously existing but unknown interests can surface.

Moreover, we created lessons designed to improve secondary students' abilities to empathize with others rather than to feel sorry for them because of their limitations. Classmates' strengths are highlighted while weaknesses are evaluated positively as areas for improvement. Many of the simulation activities and role playing lessons are designed with this second factor in mind.

As for identifying and encouraging the sharing of commonalities, most lessons provide such experiences. Debriefing of lessons provide additional opportunities for similarities between classmates to evolve. Activities requiring consensus add additional chances for commonalities to surface.

Not only does the sharing of commonalities encourage friendships for secondary students, but it assists them in the important realization that they are not totally different from their peers. In reality, they share more commonalities than differences. Through these activities they recognize that they are going through similar stages and self-identity problems. Thus, they feel more stable and get a sense of belonging within their peer groups.

Finally, most lessons in *Unlocking Doors to Self-Esteem* avoid competition and support a cooperative and cohesive classroom. Students are reinforced for working toward the common good of all their classmates. In many instances, peer feedback is used rather than teacher evaluation.

All in all, the activities in this book embody each of the above mentioned factors in such a way as to facilitate secondary students' personal growth as well as their social development.

A FRIEND

My friend is special because I can share more with him than I can with my teachers, counselor or even my parents. I can also talk and do a lot more with him than with the same people I've already mentioned. But most of all I can trust him more than anyone.

A Recipe for Friendship Is:
1/4 Trust
1/4 Compatibility
2/4 Love

Trust: Everyone needs someone whom they can trust with their hopes, dreams, and secrets.

Compatibility: You have to become compatible with your friend or you and your friend will always have fights.

Love: You have to care about that friend because if you didn't you might find one day that your friend has been run over by a car and you could say "so what!" when what they really need is you by their bedside showing your love and compassion or kindness. Don't laugh! It just might happen to you. It did to me, and my friend died.

By Jacky Ruble
Chula Vista, CA

Adolescent Friendship Formation

The challenges of adolescent social development and the factors contributing to acceptance of self and others have been pondered by many theorists. There are as many outlooks as there are branches of psychological thought, in that each theorist tends to fit adolescent development and friendship formation into his own theoretical framework. We found Erik Erikson and Jean Piaget's theories to be quite helpful as well as some current studies. A synopsis of these theories are presented here together with how they are incorporated into *Unlocking Doors to Self-Esteem.*

RECIPE FOR FRIENDSHIP FOR TWO PEOPLE

Ingredients:

2   *people*
1 *Cup of sharing*
1 *Cup of love*
1/4 *Cup of caring*
1/3 *Cup of kindness*
2   *Tablespoons of support*
1   *Tablespoon of ideas, hobbies or things in common*
1/2 *Teaspoon happiness*

Mix the sharing with the caring and stir in love.
Mix it well, for you can tell
in friendship, those aren't enough.
Now pour in kindness and the happiness;
don't forget the support.
Friendship needs all things of this sort.
Now take the people and dip them in;
dip them in their common ideas.
Now you should have friendship coming very, very soon.

By Elizabeth Cansicio
Chula Vista, CA

Erik Erikson, representing a psychoanalytical viewpoint, speaks of adolescence as a "physiological revolution" (Erikson, 1950). Adolescents' emotional and psychological growth patterns along with increased sexual awareness threaten their body images and ego identities. At this time in their lives they become preoccupied with their perception of what others think of them as compared with how they see themselves. Moreover, during this stage of development, the establishment of a positive ego identity is their prime focus. Thus, adolescents confused about their own social roles try out numerous others. They frequently over-identify with movie stars, pop singers, sports figures, and political leaders to the extent that they go off on a tangent.

Adolescents have a desperate need for social belonging and recognition. They define their own identities within the social setting in relation to their peer group. Involvement in the peer group creates a group cohesion clannish in nature. As a corollary to this clannishness, intolerance of the differences of others evolves. This new social stance is explained by Erikson as the adolescent's "defense against the dangers of self diffusion" (Muuss, 1965). Self-doubting adolescents use different or "out-group" peers as targets for their own feelings of inferiority. The contrast with the out-group's lack of acceptance seems to provide those who are included a sense of status and belonging in the group.

The goals and objectives of *Unlocking Doors to Self-Esteem* address adolescent needs of establishing positive identities and enhancing self-confidence. Included activities encourage and provide time for secondary students to feel good about themselves and their bodies in accordance with Erikson's theory. Moreover, when students have higher self-esteem, fewer of them will find it

A RECIPE FOR FRIENDSHIP

The recipe for friendship is kindness, being thoughtful, nice, treat people nice, be helpful, understand them. If you mix all of those ingredients you will have a long-lasting friendship. Also you might have lots of friends. Maybe you won't because you are too nice, kind and helpful. They might hate people like that so sometimes be a little mean here and there and maybe your enemies might be your friends for a while.

By Diane Kim
Chula Vista, CA

necessary to "pick on" or isolate their peers. Building stronger self-concepts in students is a major component of this book. Specific lessons dealing with this objective appear in Chapter IV.

Also Erikson mentions the desperate desire that occurs within adolescents to be members of a social group. Classmates provide strong group support and feedback to each other throughout the activities presented in this book. Chapter IV, "Keeping the Door Open" gives adolescents positive interaction and communication skills training, which assists them in their search for acceptance and peer group inclusion.

Another theorist offering insight into the nature of adolescent development and friendship formation was Jean Piaget. As a well known cognitive

MY FRIEND IS SPECIAL BECAUSE

To me my friend is special because she understands me. She's always there when I need her.

My friend is special to me because we share a lot of things other people don't.

We go to a lot of places. We do a lot of things together. If I had to pick another friend I couldn't find a better one than my friend.

I guess she's my best friend because she's like a sister to me. That's why she's so special to me.

By Kelly Kauffman
Chula Vista, CA

development theorist, he speaks of adolescence as a time when young people are busy acquiring a special ego-centrism with the onset of formal operational thought. This cognitive developmental stage enables adolescents to conceptualize about themselves while theorizing about the thoughts of others — something they were previously not equipped to do.

Unfortunately adolescents' speculations about others' thoughts are incorrect because they think they are the focus of those thoughts. To add to this misconception, adolescents experience alternating bouts of self criticism and self adoration. They believe their peers have these same opinions about them. Both perceptions create a personal dilemma which results in self-consciousness and reluctance to trust or reveal themselves to others.

Adolescents further believe they must be unique or extraordinary if they are of such importance to so many people. This belief often surfaces in two common actions. The first is the practice of diary or journal writing. This is done to record

the important events of their lives for posterity's sake. A person of such uniqueness should be shared with others. A second typical action of adolescents that illustrates their feeling of superiority is their overuse of the phrase, "You don't

MY FRIEND IS SPECIAL

*My friend is very special to me because he's always there
when I need him. He knows how to solve many problems that I
have.*

*When I get into a fight with another guy he's right there to
make sure no one else jumps into the fight.*

*He's special because he shows me different things or ways of
doing things like math or sports. One other reason he's special is,
he's there when I need him.*

By Ed Van Aelstyn
Chula Vista, CA

know how it feels..." (Elkind, 1974). Fortunately, according to the Cognitive
Development Theory, as the differentiation between their own thoughts and the
thoughts of others progresses, this ego-centrism dissolves.

When working with adolescents, secondary teachers will find it beneficial to
keep in mind this ego-centrism described by Piaget. The lessons in *Unlocking
Doors to Self-Esteem* do in fact encourage students to exchange feelings about
topics that affect them as well as their peers. This is to help adolescents eliminate
some of their misperceptions and fantasies about others' thoughts and their own
"uniqueness." In effect, these strategies enable secondary students to realize that
they are not alone.

In addition, training ideas are suggested for adolescents to help alleviate
some of their self-criticism and unrealistic perceptions of situations. Among the
techniques emphasized in *Unlocking Doors to Self-Esteem* are effective problem
solving and workable listening skills.

Besides building a theoretical foundation to answer the questions of adolescent friendship formations, we sought information about the factors that contribute to acceptance and inclusion at this age. We gathered our own empirical
data by administering a survey to 210 randomly selected secondary students in
Southern California. One hundred and twenty of those participating were

female, the rest being male. Results were coded and tallied to show the top 10 responses. Percentage differences in male and female responses were also recorded.

The survey questions were directed to desired personality traits sought in the formation of same sex friendships. As expected, the responses from males and females differed. Males had a difficult time answering questions relating to same sex friends. When they did, they listed athletic ability, honesty/trustworthiness,

MY FRIEND IS SPECIAL

My friend is special because he is a nice person. He likes what I like and dislikes the things I dislike. He is special because we have a lot in common and we both have the same interests in things, like sports and games.

My friend is special because I can trust him and he can trust me. We both let each other use our things without worrying that it will be lost, broken, or stolen. We both help each other out with our problems and give our point of view.

By Mike Chandler
Chula Vista, CA

responsible/mature behaviors as desired traits to be sought in friends. The females felt that good personality, same interests, sense of humor, and being kind and considerate were of prime importance.

Another aspect addressed in the survey relative to friendships revolved around the conversation topics students shared with each other. We felt this information would help us gain insight into the isolation and rejection that certain individuals experienced at this time. Also this information would be valuable in the development of the *Unlocking Doors to Self-Esteem* curriculum. Conversation topics that males mentioned the most were opposite sex, sex, and sports. Girls answering the survey named opposite sex, school, other friends, and gossip as popular topics of exchange with their friends.

In general, topics shared by girls were geared more toward private problems and life experiences, while the boys pursued "safe" topics like sports, places to go, jokes, weekends, cars, and school.

Finally, there was a survey question referring to personality traits that kept students from being accepted by their peers. For the boys responding to this question, the most important reasons given as to why one may not be liked were "causes trouble, attention-seeking, and starts fights." Other answers listed frequently were "phony," "puts on an act," "bossy," "smart mouth" and "dumb/

WAYS I'M LIKE MY CLASSMATES
(OR FEELINGS ABOUT FRIENDS)

I think that I'm like my classmates and my classmates are like me! I think they're like me because of the craziness when we are next to each other or their craziness when we are all in a group. I think it's pretty neat the way we all hang around in class and after class.

It kind of gives you a good feeling when you're all alone at nutrition break, and here come all your friends smiling, laughing, and talking. So then you're not alone, and it's not even boring. I think that's the greatest feeling you get to have in school.

It's also a great feeling to talk to your friends in class. I think they have some word for this . . . togetherness.

By Erni Barros
Chula Vista, CA

boring." Girls mentioned "stuck up," "conceited" and "snobbish." Their responses were socially oriented with "conforming to the group," "being unfriendly," "acting stupid," and "bad appearance" stated most often.

Responses to this question come into focus when secondary teachers consider the group dynamics happening at any given time in their classrooms. Students who may not be competent socially or academically often exhibit negative attention-seeking behavior in order to gain some type of recognition by those around them. The results of this survey verify that this type of behavior is not considered "cool" or accepted by the general adolescent population. Activities in *Unlocking Doors to Self-Esteem* provide students who act inappropriately with information they need to make some modifications in their behavior. At the same time the lessons suggest models of appropriateness and acceptance. Many students may know they are not doing the correct thing, but don't know how to change to make things better for themselves.

Peretti's research (1973) adds more light on how students can become more accepting to their peers. He reports that those who measure up to the expectations of their peer group are accepted. Both males and females place great emphasis on "having a good personality," "being friendly," and "being nice to other

MY FRIEND IS SPECIAL

My friend is special because she is loyal and the most honest person I know. I can talk to my special friend about subjects I couldn't or wouldn't talk about with any other person. Even though we went to different schools, and didn't see each other for more than a month, we both remained honest and best friends.

We would never lie to each other. We would never even hide the truth from each other. She can speak her point of view about me without insulting me. We are always open to each other. When we need help, and we could give the help, we do. We can go places together and have a great time. We almost always agree with each other but even if we don't, that's okay.

My special friend didn't become special in one day. We worked it up to each other in a special way. We have known each other since kindergarten, starting from a small speck and building up to a strong friendship. I'll always remember that nothing's better than a friend, but the best thing is a special friend.

By Barbara Poukkula
Chula Vista, CA

kids." Students he found to be unacceptable for peer group inclusion were ones who were listless, quiet, aggressive, socially ineffective, rebellious, fearful, and unkind.

The results of our survey, coupled with Peretti's findings, helped us to further familiarize ourselves with the problems and conflicts of social development during the age of adolescence. Developing a curriculum for the secondary level that could be infused into existing academics, while meeting the social needs of students was the ultimate challenge. Before this could be accomplished, we needed to know what strategies had already been used to eliminate the stereotypic barriers dividing students and which ones met with success. What we discovered will be presented in the next section of this chapter.

Elimination of Stereotypes

One of the major goals of *Unlocking Doors to Self-Esteem* is to provide students with opportunities to explore their feelings, attitudes and actions toward others. In doing so, it is hoped that students will begin to break down the barriers existing within their classrooms that result from preconceived stereotypes.

Allport, a leading personality theorist, has addressed the nature of prejudice and the problems of overcoming existing stereotypic barriers in our society. He mentions many techniques that have been tried in attempts to make people's attitudes more positive. They include legislation, formal educational methods, contact and acquaintance programs, mass media, group retraining, and individual therapy (Allport, 1960).

Zeroing in on formal educational approaches, he found numerous methods that have been tried within schools and are considered to facilitate positive attitude changes. Some of these are classified as direct methods where the students are aware of what's happening to them; while others are indirect methods that attempt to change prejudicial attitudes in a "round about" manner.

The information method is one example of a direct approach. In this method — used widely in many subject areas, particularly social science units — teachers approach a particular population head on, attempting to inform their students in an objective, knowledge-acquiring way. The informational method is considered by many to be an indispensible forerunner to some of the other methods. Their reasoning is that without intercultural information obtained at school, students have limited opportunities to learn in an objective way about people who are different from them. Accurate information is viewed as a probable ally to improved relationships (Allport, 1960).

An example of an indirect approach effective in changing attitudes provides students with vicarious experiences in which they may view certain films, read novels, or act in plays designed to encourage a sympathetic identification. For example, when students view a film such as "Elephant Man," they realize that the elephant man is human and also has feelings. Consequently, they can identify with the character. In turn, they begin to generalize their newly-acquired empathy toward people they may know with different problems.

Allport mentions another educational method that uses both the direct and indirect approaches depending on the activities involved. The participation method can send students into neighborhoods to get actively involved in festivals or community projects. This is direct experience in that the students are aware of what they are to do and why they are there.

24

If done within the school, however, where students are grouped and collaborate with each other in pursuit of some common goal, such as a school fair or play, the students are not totally aware of what's happening. In effect, this indirect approach aids in developing positive new acquaintances with others who are members of an unfamiliar group. The results of these experiences are summed up by Allport's statement, (1960), "prejudice tends to diminish whenever members of different groups meet on terms of equal status in pursuit of common objectives" (p. 246).

In general, most theorists agree that when one tries to change attitudes in an indirect manner, students will benefit more than from the direct approach. As a result, positive change occurs. Students tend to gain when they immerse themselves in community projects and participate in realistic situations. These methods are non-threatening and non-forced. They help students develop an *acquaintance with* rather than a *knowledge of* the unfamiliar culture or out-person.

A study by Ziegler supports this indirect approach for attitude change. Using a field method approach to observe inter-ethnic friendship patterns in four different schools, Ziegler noted that greater inter-ethnic contact occurred in schools that had students from more diverse backgrounds. His suggestion was that teachers structure inter-ethnic contact into their daily classroom curriculum to enable students to become acquainted with each other as opposed to just learning about one another (Ziegler, 1979).

A forerunner of *Unlocking Doors to Self-Esteem* which also takes both approaches into consideration is Fox's *Communicating to Make Friends* (CMF) (1980). The CMF program effectively facilitates positive interaction and social acceptance among elementary age students of various races, cultures, and sexes. Although not written for secondary students, it has been utilized and found successful for this population. The program encourages unfamiliar classmates to get acquainted by discovering and discussing their commonalities. A unique feature of the CMF Program that adds to its effectiveness is the progression of weekly activities. They are structured as a natural friendship would occur. This practice insures the positiveness of the newly forming social relationships between particular partners as well as among all classmates. The first third of the program has participants involved in sharing non-threatening factual information about themselves. As time evolves, partners are then asked to share personal information of a higher level, i.e., mutual interests. Finally, students reach the stage of sharing feelings.

In *Unlocking Doors to Self-Esteem* we used primarily indirect approaches to meet our goals. Infusing the social objective into the daily subject area unit, while students remain unaware, is an example of this approach. Self-concept, attitude change, and interpersonal communications do not exist as separate units. Instead they are indirectly dealt with in books, classroom discussions, group tasks and assignments, and methods of presentation.

Specifically, "Learning from the Media" and "Handicaps Don't Have to be Limiting" are examples of lessons that use vicarious experiences to promote a sympathetic identification from students. In the first, a drama activity, students are encouraged to view contemporary films having a multi-cultural emphasis as well as films that deal with discrimination issues such as age, sex, and the handicapped. Class discussions and field trips are suggested. In the second example, students interview a guest speaker who has a handicap or particular limitation that has been overcome. In both activities, students are looking in from the outside but gaining a sympathetic understanding.

In the career education activity, "Get the Job Done," a participation method is used. Students are sent into the community to interview workers in certain positions. They note particulars about the environment and what skills are necessary for the job. Later, students come back to class, where they analyze and suggest modifications that could be made for an employee possessing a certain limitation. In effect, they must try to come up with a workable solution for the inclusion of this person.

All of these techniques help familiarize students from diverse backgrounds with each other. They also highlight similarities, cooperation, and positive interaction.

Successful Learning Strategies

In addition to the development of activities that promote the growth of self-confidence and the elimination of stereotypic barriers, we sought to provide lessons that would facilitate students in their quest for stronger interpersonal relationships. To accomplish these objectives in the most efficient and effective manner, we studied existing successful learning theories for direction.

The Modeling Theory of Albert Bandura provided welcome direction (Bandura, 1971; Bandura & Walters, 1963). Bandura's research shows that students learn very effectively from observing the behavior of their peers. After a new behavior pattern is observed, it soon becomes incorporated into the observer's own monitoring system. Of the two other learning strategies reviewed — shaping and coaching — modeling techniques were found to be more effective and less time-consuming (O'Connor, 1972). The latter aspect added extra credence to its usage in *Unlocking Doors to Self-Esteem*.

Throughout the book, numerous opportunities are available for teachers and students to see desirable social patterns modeled. However, peer modeling is stressed in accordance with the adolescent social developmental patterns discussed earlier in this chapter.

Another reason for utilizing the modeling approach lies in providing direction for helping socially isolated students. Many of these individuals exhibit antisocial behaviors, either consciously or unconsciously, that have become habits and the only ones they know. By creating opportunities for them to see their classmates acting appropriately, they can learn new behaviors. Many of the included activities also help clarify exactly what is expected for acceptance within their peer subculture.

As we sought answers to the questions relative to why people are attracted to each other, how adolescents form their friendships, how to eliminate stereotypic barriers, and what teaching techniques are effective — the foundations of *Unlocking Doors to Self-Esteem* evolved. Using this information and applying it to the structure of the secondary classroom, we constructed a workable tool for use by secondary teachers. Successful field testing and evaluations reinforced and solidified the concepts in the book.

THE MASTER KEY:

THE TEACHER

CHAPTER III

THE MASTER KEY: THE TEACHER

Chapter III

In order for teachers to help their students meet the goals of *Unlocking Doors to Self-Esteem*, it is important for them to determine how well they are modeling what they are teaching. This chapter will assist teachers with their self-evaluations as well as provide ideas for modification. More specifically, directions are presented to enable teachers to accomplish for themselves the same three goals they have set for their students:

1. Teachers will explore the alternatives and suggestions given to strengthen their self-awareness and self-concept.
2. Teachers will explore their own attitudes, feelings and actions toward others while working to eliminate stereotypic and social barriers.
3. Teachers will examine their own skills for promoting positive relationships with their students and colleagues.

To be a successful change agent in areas as important as personal and social growth requires more than just doing a few lessons. The real change evolves when the teacher and classroom atmosphere model and support the social concept of the lesson. As stated by Fox and Malian (1983) the best place to begin in the accomplishment of these goals is with the *TEACHER*.

A Very Important Person

Before teachers can help their students develop healthy, positive self-concepts, they must feel good about themselves. Educators must be confident in their abilities as well as aware and accepting of their strengths and weaknesses. Unfortunately, not all teachers feel praiseworthy. This chapter examines some of the obstacles that prevent teachers from feeling successful. Suggestions to facilitate overcoming these barriers and to improve teachers' self-esteem are also included.

Numerous concerns are necessary in protecting and enhancing teachers' self-concepts. First, teachers need to take special care of their physical needs. Due to the nature of the teaching profession, teachers come into continual contact with sick students, making them very vulnerable to illness. If the teacher's health is poor, it can overshadow everything. Thus, teachers should take extra measures to

GETTING TO KNOW ME

Getting to know me isn't as hard
*   as it sounds.*
I'm not set by any special bounds.
I've achieved all my goals.
I've jumped over those holes.
I've reached for the star
*   and found it wasn't far.*
And forever through the thick and the thin,
I always knew I was going to win.

By Cheryl Jennings
San Diego, CA

insure regular exercise, proper diet, and relaxation to prevent illness.

Another area of concern is mental stress. Stress can be a realistic consequence of pedagogy, and teachers often suffer because of the pressures they put on themselves or those caused by the reactions of others.

If teachers are not well-organized or in control of their classrooms, a stress problem will occur and perpetuate itself. When this is the case, teachers should not be afraid to do some self-evaluation. Requesting help from fellow faculty members or district personnel may assist teachers in revitalizing their teaching styles or behavior management skills. Often participating in a workshop or taking an additional university course can help them improve these skills; adding new techniques to their repertoire. These actions usually result in relieving personal and teacher-related forms of stress.

On the other hand, the stress may be caused by something that teachers cannot control. If this is so, educators should be flexible and consider a possible change of environment or career. A new beginning often provides teachers with some challenging alternatives and newly acquired support.

Sometimes stress is caused by administrative personnel or by the principal. A realistic evaluation of the legitimacy of the criticism or suggestion should then take place. Teachers should do this, keeping in mind that the employer is not attacking their person, but objectively judging their performance. Too often constructive and helpful suggestions are misunderstood and thought to be personal attacks. If teachers feel confident and capable in their skills and abilities, they are not likely to misunderstand the well-meaning suggestions of other professionals. On the other hand, teachers should not feel uncomfortable standing up against criticism they feel is unjust.

HOW TO REACT

Should I cry and shout,
or be shy and pout?

Should I grin so big and smile
you could see it for a mile?

Should I say "Congratulations!"
or turn and walk away?

Of course I'll go and say

"Thank you, I've learned a lot this day."

By Tara Nicholson
Oceanside, CA

There are many forces in society making negative judgments relative to the educational process and too often blaming teachers for ailments that exist. Against this non-supportive background, it is difficult for good educators to believe in themselves and support a healthy positive self-concept. Teachers need to become more assertive, standing up for their rights and their profession. Most teachers are dedicated, well-trained, and capable. A public relations campaign is suggested. Educators should not be afraid to let the community know of the positive things that are happening in their classrooms. It's okay to publicize their accomplishments and be proud of them.

Taking charge of one's life and being assertive are important components of teaching. There are numerous classes teachers can attend and books to read that can help them to feel and act capable. The success of the *Assertive Discipline Program* by Lee Canter (1976) is a prime example of how teachers can learn to control their own destiny as well as their classroom.

Along with taking care of themselves and learning to be assertive, teachers are encouraged to reward themselves whenever they experience success, however large or small. They should take time to enjoy it personally and share it with others.

Many things can and should be done to facilitate a positive faculty climate and help teachers and administrators share in each others' accomplishments. People need to be recognized. One way to do this is to set up a bulletin board in the front office or faculty lounge displaying the "good work of teachers." This practice can be done on a regular basis for the teaching staff, administrators, and other school personnel.

Principals and administrators were included in the above ideas because their recognition will benefit them as well as their staff. It will model what needs to be done by them for their faculty members as well as enhance their self-concepts. If everyone is reinforced, professional performance will improve.

This section has focused on presenting some of the ingredients that facilitate a positive self-esteem for teachers. Although teachers know the importance of these ideas for their students, they often forget about their own needs. We want to reiterate the importance of teacher self-confidence and to provide teachers with ideas for taking care of themselves. Only then will they be able to truly understand and meet their students' needs.

A Model of Acceptance

Once teachers begin to feel good about themselves as human beings and start to see themselves as competent, it is important for them to evaluate their

I LOVE YOU

I thought I could never
touch a bird flying high
Nor watch all the cars
on the road pass me by.
You've taken the time
to lend me your hand,
You've brought me to the beach
just to lie on the sand.
You've taught me so many things —
things I should know
About growing up
and places to go.
You are my special friend
Just want you to know
I love you so much
for letting me go.

By Melinda Macaspac
San Diego, CA

attitudes, feelings, and actions toward their students and colleagues. To encourage their students to accept others, teachers must make sure they are feeling and demonstrating acceptance of these same individuals. The easiest way to guarantee this is for teachers to work toward acceptance of all students. This practice must be taken seriously so that teachers are truly modeling a personal commitment to eliminate the stereotypes and social barriers perpetuated by our society.

This goal is often difficult to reconcile for most individuals, including teachers. However, teachers should consider learning ways in which they can objectively evaluate the stereotypes they are perpetuating. Further, they need to develop a plan to eliminate their own negative attitudes. This action is especially important because teachers come into direct contact with so many consciousness-developing young individuals. Students are very definitely influenced by their teachers' attitudes and actions. In many cases, students take on their teachers' thoughts and make them their own. Thus, it is important for teachers to make sure they are modeling appropriate attitudes.

Unfortunately, many teachers are unaware of their attitudes. As a case in point, how often do teachers, while in the lounge or at lunch, make racial or cultural remarks or jokes about other staff members, students, or the population in general? How often do regular educators talk about special education students and teachers in less than understanding and accepting terms? Unfortunately, these negative conversations do exist, and in many situations these attitudes and opinions don't end here. Teachers, without consciously realizing it, carry these thoughts and words into actions into their classrooms. Usually, it's done in very subtle ways. Unfortunately, what happens is that students read these actions and often adopt them.

An example of how subtle these messages can be is demonstrated in the situation where a social science teacher is giving a lesson on appreciating other cultures with all the appropriate reasons. At the same time, this teacher has a Cambodian student in the class with whom he really feels frustrated because the student has difficulty in speaking or understanding the English language. The teacher, even during the lesson, doesn't provide any opportunity for this student to share his culture. What students are hearing about appreciating is being negated by what their teacher is doing in reality. They will focus on the actions rather than the words.

We are bringing this negative possibility to light in order to help teachers become more sensitive to what they are saying as well as doing. In the case of the Cambodian student, what did that teacher do to this student's self-esteem? Also, did the teacher make any contribution to breaking down social barriers?

It is difficult to discuss these issues because most people are guilty of violating them. However, they must be brought out into the open so strategies for change can be planned and implemented. More specifically, once teachers as well as members of society realize that there is a problem, they can learn to monitor themselves.

Before going on to the last goal of this chapter, we present one more example of a realistic situation reinforcing the importance of teachers modeling acceptance. Although the example focuses on handicapped students, the concepts of awareness and acceptance can be generalized to apply to all people who have been ostracized.

The following two situations focus on how two teachers handled the same problem. Notice how they perceived the situation, their attitudes, and their subsequent actions.

Mrs. Jones learned that she will have a girl with cerebral palsy mainstreamed into her anatomy class during fourth period. Her first reaction is fear. She has never really known or even talked to a person in a wheelchair. Also, she's really not sure what cerebral palsy is. Her limited knowledge recalls that people with this condition have uncontrollable jerking and their balance is off. She has also heard that sometimes a person with cerebral palsy can't talk very well and may drool. She doesn't know what to expect and is afraid to seek information for fear that she will seem ignorant on the subject as well as not being open to having a mainstreamed student in her class. Negative thoughts and feelings of doubt run through her mind all week.

By the time Janet, the CP student arrives, Mrs. Jones is very uncomfortable. She does her duty as a "good" teacher and welcomes Janet with all the proper words, however, her body language reveals her real feelings of inadequacy. She has difficulty giving eye contact to Janet and is unable to bring herself to touch the shoulder of this girl in a wheelchair whose neck is turned to one side. She feels bad because she knows that many of her other students enjoy the physical contact or touches of reinforcement she gives them.

Not only does she realize her inadequacy; so do her students. They have the same feelings and uncertainties, having never experienced interacting with a handicapped person. Mrs. Jones, her students, and Janet never feel comfortable with one another because of their first experiences. What does occur subsequently is that Janet's classmates never accept her as an equal but seem to pity and feel sorry for her.

Throughout the remainder of the year Mrs. Jones did the best she could but never was able to feel relaxed around Janet. Thus they all missed the opportunity to make a valuable friend and learn something from one another.

Now let's look at the same situation and see how it could be modified to make everyone more comfortable, as well as taking positive steps toward eliminating stereotypical and social barriers about the handicapped.

Mr. Smith hears that he will be getting a new student. The student has cerebral palsy and has been in a special education class for three months at his school. Mr. Smith realizes he knows very little about handicapped students of any type. However, he is willing to learn and wants to help his new student succeed in his class. Not knowing what to expect and realizing his uncomfortable feelings, Mr. Smith contacts the special education teacher. Together they decide it would be a good idea for him to visit the special education classroom to see what these students are doing as well as to meet Janet, his soon-to-be student.

Mr. Smith is a little nervous about the visit but goes, and is very surprised to discover that many of these students are capable academically as well as easy to talk to. He and Janet hit it off well as Janet is able to show Mr. Smith what she *can* do. Their conversation allows Mr. Smith to ask Janet or her teacher about things he doesn't know or understand. Also, the special education teacher gives Mr. Smith some specific ideas for helping Janet integrate academically and socially into his classroom.

Mr. Smith immediately goes back to his class and shares his experience and new knowledge. The class is receptive and decides they want to know more about Janet and also her cerebral palsy. Since Mr. Smith teaches anatomy, he feels it would be meaningful for his students to do some research on some common physiological problems such as cerebral palsy. After his students research their topics, they decided that it might be a good idea to do some planning for Janet's arrival.

Finally, when Janet arrives, she is truly welcomed by Mr. Smith and the students. They spend the class period getting to know one another, sharing their research, and asking Janet some questions. They are off to a good start.

The second situation illustrates how stereotypes can be eliminated as well as how teachers can model and encourage acceptance of others. Mr. Smith showed his respect for Janet by treating her as he would have liked to have been treated himself. He also learned that pity and sympathy were different from empathy and was able to model this for his students. Finally, he didn't let his negative feelings stand in the way of taking some positive steps to change them.

An Active Participant

Having discussed ideas for improving teachers' self-concepts and presenting thoughts on eliminating stereotypes, it's time to consider how teachers can become active participants in their classrooms. It is vital that secondary teachers recognize adolescents have difficulty accepting authority. In their search for social identity, students tend to reject anyone who makes demands on them, especially if the demand conflicts with their perceptions of themselves and others. Because of this identity crisis, adolescents are more sensitive about the actions and reactions of those around them, especially their peers. This is a time when peer pressure is at its strongest. With these factors in mind, let's look at ways secondary teachers can avoid alienating themselves from their students. These practices will be helpful in relationships with others as well.

An important part of getting to know others is the willingness to open the doors by being the person who initiates the interaction. When working with adolescents, often it's the teacher who is put into the role of the initiator. Thus, it is of prime importance that the teacher begins the relationship in such a manner as to encourage continued communication.

We will not detail improving communication skills, but will present a few ideas relating directly to communicating with adolescents. In addition, we refer teachers to two excellent works that provide detailed strategies for evaluating and enhancing skills in this area:

Gordon, T. and Burch, N. *Teacher Effectiveness Training.*
New York: Peter H. Wyden Publishers, 1974.
Ginott, H.G. *Teacher and Child: A Book for Parents and Teachers.* New York: The MacMillan Company, 1972.

Given the sensitivity of adolescents' social and emotional development, secondary teachers might make a special effort to avoid demands that could be interpreted by their students as commands. This helps to eliminate the need for students to confront their teachers and close communication channels. Some alternatives that will facilitate their growth and at the same time show them they are respected and accepted by their teachers are as follows:

1) When planning class activities, it is helpful to keep in mind that adolescents are primarily focused on meeting their social needs.
2) Provide students with opportunities to experience their independence. Give them choices in class relative to the topics they will be studying, times they'll be studying, and how they'll be learning — as well as demonstrating their knowledge of the subject. This can be done easily by encouraging their involvement in some of the planning. They'll be much more receptive if they are involved.
3) Rather than telling students what to do, present your needs and the situation in such a manner that the students offer support. The use of problem solving techniques can be modeled as well as reinforced by using this strategy.
4) Students can benefit greatly from studying the problem solving model by Thomas Gordon in *Parent Effectiveness Training* (1975). This approach will be useful both in and out of class when a consensus is required.

5) Teachers who show their willingness to cooperate and to value the opinions of their students receive respect and cooperation in return.
6) One way to illustrate respect for students is to avoid embarrassing or labeling them in a negative way in front of their peers even when they are behaving inappropriately. Counsel or discipline students in a private and confidential place.
7) Although part of teaching is providing students with academic feedback, it's important that the feedback is presented in such a manner that it suggests guidance and direction rather than criticism. Choice of wording either orally or in writing should be analyzed and modified to convey positiveness. Describe the areas of improvement rather than evaluate them.

Teachers can further enhance their effectiveness as participants in their classrooms by doing some self-evaluation of non-verbal ways in which they communicate, particularly their body language. Once again the interactions of teachers with their students will be discussed to present this concept, however the ideas can be generalized to all relationships.

Teachers often verbalize one thing and demonstrate the opposite with their eyes and/or bodies. An example in point is Mr. Thomas, the environmental science teacher, who had his students do an activity where they shared impressions on pollution. He chose not to involve himself in the activity as was his common response.

Observing Mr. Thomas more closely, it appears that he avoids interaction with his students. A non-biased observer might record the following actions to explain how Mr. Thomas projects such an unwelcoming image.

Mr. Thomas always stands behind his desk or lectern when addressing the class. Students are always sitting while he is standing. When he speaks to his students individually, Mr. Thomas' arms are usually folded in front of him or on his hips. However, he *tells* his students that he treats them as adults.

What message *is* he conveying to his students? Students think that he sees himself as "above" interacting with them. He is "too good" or too uncomfortable to let them know him as a person. It does not matter what he says — students shy away from him, and he is viewed as the authoritarian.

If Mr. Thomas did some self-evaluation or discussed this with a fellow faculty member, he would find he is projecting the opposite of what he wants or says he wants. Although this teacher is in the habit of sending out unwelcoming body language, there are things he can do to change his patterns. First, he could sit next to students when he talks to them. He could walk around the table or lectern throughout his presentation to get closer to his students, effectively showing his comfort with their presence. This is an especially good technique to use when trying to get students involved in the presentation, too.

Another suggestion he should consider is to become an active participant in group activities that involve everyone sharing. He could model what he wants as well as share his personal thoughts, making him an integral part of the class. He might also model acceptance by positioning himself with different students when he does interact.

In order to convey an air of interest, concern, and openness, Mr. Thomas could monitor the position of his arms and hands more closely. He could also provide eye contact with his students. Both gestures demonstrate genuine interest in what the other person is saying or doing, thus opening the doors to quality interaction.

Listening effectively is a useful skill for secondary teachers. Their students need and appreciate having contact with an adult model who listens and genuinely tries to understand. However, learning to listen well is difficult. It requires the receiver of information to concentrate on what the speaker is saying. It involves analyzing his feelings as well as the words he is using. Through effective listening, the receiver can convey acceptance, empathy, and a desire to deal with the situation at hand. Good listeners avoid making judgments relative to the speaker. If done properly, listening can also provide the receiver with opportunities to open doors of communication allowing the speaker to share more about himself. This shared information can help teachers gain insight into their students' personal and educational needs.

Secondary teachers are role-models for their adolescent students in numerous ways, including communication skills. One of their major instructional goals should be to constantly remind themselves of their influence on their students. If they do this they will be opening the doors to better teacher/student relationships. They will be growing personally and professionally as their students benefit from their example.

Things to Come

Ideas for self-concept enhancement have been presented, together with strategies for becoming a more accepting role model. In addition, some methods for expanding personal involvement between teachers and their students have been identified in this chapter.

However, it is the implementation of these suggestions that will assist teachers of secondary students in becoming effective MASTER KEYS in the social and emotional development of their students. Once they have performed some self-evaluation and completed the necessary positive modifications, they are ready to work with their students in accomplishing similar goals.

The rest of *Unlocking Doors to Self-Esteem* concentrates on providing educators with over one hundred lessons and units of study to aid them in this challenge. These lessons begin in Chapter IV and continue through Chapter VI. They will assist teachers in opening doors to friendship and developing positive communication between adolescents in their classrooms.

A SPECIAL DOOR:

DEVELOPING POSITIVE SELF CONCEPTS

CHAPTER IV

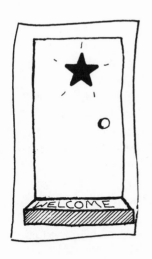
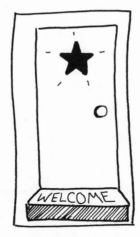
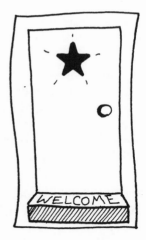

A SPECIAL DOOR: DEVELOPING POSITIVE SELF-CONCEPTS

Chapter IV

This chapter presents ideas and resources to provide successful experiences for students which in turn will help enhance their self-concepts. Before teachers begin to implement the suggested lessons and units of study, there are some effective practices that can be done with students in all subject areas.

Given that classrooms are composed of students of diverse backgrounds, abilities, and needs, there are numerous things teachers can do to provide their students with opportunities for success academically, behaviorally, and socially. One way to assure this success is to have realistic expectations of what students can and cannot do in each of these growth areas. Having realistic expectations does not mean lowered expectations for some students or thinking that a particular student is not able to perform with the rest of the class. It is very important for teachers to look at each student as a potential "winner" and identify areas in which he/she is capable. When this is done, teachers can explore helpful resources that enable their students to perform at their highest potential. This practice is particularly important to use with mainstreamed students from special education classes or those who have limited English speaking skills. It's important to look for the best and to avoid incorrect assumptions based on myths or misunderstandings. Students should receive "the benefit of the doubt."

Another action that will enhance the self-concept of each student is for teachers to identify characteristics, abilities, and skills that each individual student has that can be used to represent him/her in a positive light. In addition to improving the student's self-concept this practice illustrates to the student's peers that this person is capable and has definite strengths. It is very useful to play down weaknesses, although they should never be forgotten. It helps to look at weaknesses in terms of areas of improvement rather than negative attributes. Both of these strategies will model an accepting attitude toward all students and contribute to building stronger self-esteem for them.

I SHALL OVERCOME
Conquering Your Flaws and Limitations

Subject: English   **Grade Level:** Junior High

Content Objective: Students will improve their reading comprehension skills. They will recognize basic literary elements such as characters, plot, setting, and theme.

Social Objective: Students will acquire a greater awareness of their own strengths and weaknesses.

Materials:
- Library books

Directions:
1. Have the students determine some weaknesses or limitations they feel they have. Some background activities in this area may be necessary depending on the maturity level of your students. Perhaps a filmstrip on an individual who has overcome his limitation would be beneficial. Also, if the teacher shares with the class a limitation or obstacle that he/she has conquered, this may help to introduce the lesson and break the ice.

2. Once this is identified, have students go to the library and find a book about an individual who has overcome a similar problem. It is a good idea for the teacher to be prepared with some title suggestions. Please refer to our annotated bibliography of young adult fiction in Chapter VII. They should read the book and identify the components that meet the content objectives mentioned above.

3. Have them report on the book either by a written report or an oral presentation.

4. Complete the assignment by having them develop a plan for conquering their chosen limitation.

Time: One week or as an extended homework assignment.

Notes to Teacher: An atmosphere of caring and non-judgmental acceptance will facilitate better self-exploration by the students.

POETRY WITH MEANING

Subject: English   **Grade Level:** Jr. & Sr. High

Content Objective: Students will recognize and analyze the many forms of poetry. They will create and edit their own writings, thus demonstrating effective application of their creative and communication skills. They will also identify poetic devices and terminology.

Social Objective: Students will relate the meaning of poetry to their own experience and cultures. This activity provides a medium to express feelings about oneself and others.

Materials:
• paper
• pencil

Directions: When introducing different forms of poetry (e.g., narrative, sonnet, lyric, Haiku) have students write a poem about themselves. Topics such as the following may be used:

A Reflection of Me	Looking At My Life
Getting High on Me	Me, Myself, and I
Changes I Have Gone Through	Limitations I Have Overcome
Handicaps that I Have	Ways I Am Like My Classmates
Things in my Environment that Affect Me	Things I Can Do

Time: One to two class periods

Notes to Teacher: Giving students a topic that they know something about helps make poetry more relevant to daily life. Poetry is a good productive outlet for one to reflect and express negative and positive feelings.

LIMITATIONS I HAVE OVERCOME

The limitation I think I have overcome is shyness. When I was younger I was very shy. I didn't talk very much, and if I did, kids would be surprised. Yet, now I think I've overcome that; I talk more and seem outgoing. Sometimes I even talk too much so I try not to. I am still shy about some things such as meeting new people and talking to guys, but I think all people are shy about those ideas.

By Elizabeth Cansicio, Chula Vista, CA

"ME" BASKET

Subject: English   **Grade Level:** Junior High

**Content
Objective:** The student will understand the concept of an action verb.

**Social
Objective:** Students will have the chance to explore themselves and share with others what they like to do. Similar hobbies will surface.

Materials:
- used cardboard ice cream bins from local ice cream shop
- old magazines to cut up   • scissors
- glue   • paint brushes
- clear shellac or polyurethane spray

Directions: Group students, making sure that friends are not sitting together. Students should share magazines and materials in this manner. They should be allowed to talk about what they like to do, and to cut out pictures from magazines depicting things that they enjoy doing. An emphasis is put on action verbs. The pictures are then painted onto the ice cream bin with a mixture of 50 percent white glue and 50 percent water. A nice way to do it is to overlap the pictures in a collage format. When the ice cream bin dries, it can be preserved with clear shellac or polyurethane spray.

Time: One to two class periods

**Notes to
Teacher:**
A. This activity enables grammar concepts to come alive and be introduced in another modality which helps the special education as well as regular student.

B. Students will have a chance to explore themselves and focus in on common interests.

C. "Me" baskets can be used for individual storage in school or can be taken home to enhance the atmosphere of students' bedrooms, etc.

COMP TIME FOR ME

Subject:	English

Grade Level: Jr. & Sr. High

Content Objective: Students will write a composition supporting a given topic, using clear and effective English.

Social Objective: This activity will help students pinpoint positive experiences in their lives. This in turn helps them connect with their feelings about themselves. Students will identify their positive characteristics.

Materials: • paper • pencil

Directions: When making assignments for compositions, give students a choice from the following list:

1. What are the major events in your life that have influenced your feelings about yourself? Were these positive or negative? Which ones did you have control over? Which ones didn't you have control over?

2. Looking back into your childhood, identify a person who influenced you in a positive way. Explain how he/she influenced you and why this made such a lasting impression.

3. Share one positive attribute or characteristic about yourself that you are proud of. How does this affect others?

These questions may be used as a springboard for your ideas to help foster positive self-concepts and give students an opportunity to share.

Time: Two to three class periods

Notes to Teacher:

A. Before starting this project, it might be beneficial to have students do a time line of their life, listing major events. This requires a sequence of events and at the same time presents a visual representation. This chart could also be an impetus for other composition topics.

B. If your current literature is conducive, select a story to read prior to this activity that deals with a major event over which the character does have control. Discuss the subject of control of our own lives prior to the composition writing.

C. If students have a difficult time getting started, brainstorming in groups, depending on the question, might be profitable. This will hopefully give more confidence to those who are having trouble beginning.

46

ME, MYSELF AND I

Me, myself, and I
are three persons in one body,
Each striving to find the other.

All of them are different
Yet all are of the same;
They don't know each other—or do they?

One bright, happy, carefree;
The other serious, demanding;
The third confused, scared, angry.

But at least Me, Myself, and I
Know who we are: We're special!

By Julie Peckham, San Diego, CA

47

DESCRIBING ME

Subject: English   **Grade Level:** Jr. & Sr. High

**Content
Objective:** Students will demonstrate knowledge of the concepts of the Parts of Speech. Adjectives, verbs, or nouns can be used.

**Social
Objective:** The activity fosters positive self-concepts for students.

Materials:
- paper   • pencil   • worksheet or index cards
- stencils   • crayons   • colored pencils
- marking pens   • rulers

Optional: • vocabulary building books   • dictionary   • thesaurus

Directions: Direct students to write their names vertically with large letters on a piece of paper. Next to each letter, instruct students to write an adjective that describes them and begins with that letter. For example:

Loving   Friendly

Youthful   Responsible

Noteworthy   Active

Nice   Natural

Resource books may be used if ideas are needed. Also, teacher and students can brainstorm words on the blackboard prior to executing this activity.

Time: One-half class period.

**Notes to
Teacher:**
A. When assigning this task, ask them to use only positive descriptions!

B. This could be a group activity or a get-acquainted activity.

C. This activity is invaluable to the teacher as a source of information on how the students actually view themselves.

D. This activity should be used to reinforce grammar concepts in the already existing curriculum. A class review might be needed prior to beginning.

WAYS I AM DIFFERENT

The ways I am different from the rest of this English class is that I am probably one of the worst students here. One of the reasons I think I'm not as good a student as the rest of this class is that I am a student athlete. Most of the rest of this class are just students. The sport I'm in is basketball. Most of the people in this class like sports such as baseball or football.

Another reason I am different from the rest of this class is that I was not in English honors the first semester. Only a couple of other people weren't in the honors class last semester. I'm not the kind of person that can sit at a desk for 50 minutes and write something like vocabulary work or any kind of assignment that takes a lot of sitting in one place and writing or reading. The only exception to reading would be if it was a very good book. These are the three main reasons I think I am different from the rest of the class.

By Albert Lacson
Chula Vista, CA

MY PAST, PRESENT
AND FUTURE ACTIONS

Subject: English   **Grade Level:** Jr. & Sr. High

Content Objective: Students will identify the past, present, and future tense of verbs. They will demonstrate the ability to sequence personal experiences and ideas.

Social Objective: Students will self evaluate who they are, where they've been and where they are going. Students will problem-solve goals in their own lives.

Materials:
• chalk

Directions:

1. Present Tense Example: Instruct students to think about all the things that they are doing at this exact moment. Have a class discussion and brainstorm on the blackboard. More than likely students will produce present participle forms such as:

   I am talking.   I am sitting.

   I am listening.   I am hearing.

2. Have students look at the verbs that described their actions to see if there is anything three or more students had in common. Explain to the students, when they are talking or writing that this is the present progressive form of the verb.

3. Compare this to other present forms of the verbs.

Time: One-half to whole class period

Notes to Teacher:

A. This activity produces an informal outlet for students to share and compare past experiences as well as future plans. It provides a personal touch to subject matter that would otherwise be very dry.

B. Supplementary Resources: *If You Don't Know Where You're Going, You'll Never Get There.* (Argus Publishers)

LAUGHING AT OURSELVES
CAN BE FUNNY

Subject:	English **Grade Level:** Jr. & Sr. High

Content Objective: Students will develop the ability to sequence ideas as a precursor to paragraph writing.

Social Objective: This activity will help students shed a positive light and sense of humor on their own strengths and weaknesses.

Materials:
- colored markers
- paper cut into strips 4¼" x 11" *or*
- worksheet with comic strip format already set up for students to fill in appropriate conversation.

Directions:
1. Have students design a comic strip about something that they want to improve about themselves. Let them make fun of themselves and learn to look at weaknesses in a humorous light. Then they can share their comics with classmates and laugh.

2. Pair classmates. Direct them to share some ideas for improving themselves in the area illustrated in their comics.

3. Ask students to write one or two paragraphs on what they would improve about themselves. Have them tell why and how they would go about making the improvement.

Time: One to two class periods

Notes to Teacher: An outcome of this activity is to help students realize that all people have their strengths and weaknesses and that it is okay not to be perfect.

THE MANY MOODS OF ME

I have many moods. One of my moods is happiness. If I have a good day I'm happy. If something good happens to me I feel happy.

Another mood of mine is sadness. I feel sad when I have a bad day or something goes wrong. Sometimes I don't even know why I am sad. I just am.

Sometimes I'm happy, sad, kind, and mean all together. It depends on the kind of day I've had and how I feel.

Sometimes my life gets me down. I hear of all the crimes and murders and I feel bad. I wish there were more good people in this world.

Everybody has many moods inside of them. I wish they could write them all down on a piece of paper like me.

By Kelly Kauffman
Chula Vista, CA

THE MANY MOODS OF _____

Subject: Drama & Communications   **Grade Level:** Jr. & Sr. High

Content Objective: Students will become aware of the many facets of play production other than acting (e.g. choreography).

Social Objective: Students will express feelings of confidence, as well as recognize their abilities to communicate with their bodies and faces.

Materials: • record player   • records   • stage in front of class

Directions:

1. In order to set the stage for this activity, ask students to write down ten adjectives that describe themselves.

2. Instruct students to find a record that would relay the overall feelings that they listed. This can be done for homework over the course of a week.

3. Utilizing the music, and realistically looking at themselves, have students individually create a routine (2-5 minutes) which they will perform for the group.

4. Students should be encouraged to use interesting dance routines or facial expressions without actually talking themselves.

5. While the class is observing, have them come up with five (5) descriptors for that person. Compare the individual's original list and the classmates' conclusions for evaluation.

6. Questions that can be used for discussion:

   a. Did your peers perceive you the way you intended to be perceived?

   b. If not, where are the discrepancies?

Time: Two or three class periods

Notes to Teacher: If the class is shy, divide the sexes for this activity.
Or
Discussion questions can be written on a handout for written response.

GETTING TO KNOW YOU

Subject: Drama and Communications   **Grade Level:** Junior High

Content Objective: This activity will encourage students to demonstrate their creative abilities.

Social Objective: Puppets are used as a medium to explore students' self-concepts.

Materials:
- Puppet theatre — can be constructed from old voting booths or refrigerator boxes.
- Puppets that look like the students.

Directions:
1. Pair students up. Have them introduce themselves to each other through their puppets.

   Information to share is:

   a. Name and nickname
   b. Area in which they live
   c. Classes that they are taking
   d. Things they do outside of school
   e. Favorites
   f. See if the two puppets can find at least two things they have in common.

2. Divide class into four sections. Partners will then be responsible for introducing each other using the information previously learned. Have four introductions going on at one time.

Time: One to two class periods.

Notes to Teacher:
A. This is a good introductory activity for the beginning of the year, semester, or unit.
B. Puppets can be as elaborate as individual teacher may desire. They can be made of paper bags, spoons, socks, paper plates, hands, etc. Your art teacher on campus might have some good ideas!
C. Students will take this activity as seriously as their teacher does.

PRETTY BABY / PRETTY FACE

Subject: Drama & Communications **Grade Level:** Jr. & Sr. High

Content Objective: Students will learn the basic rudiments of make-up for the purpose of theatrical enhancement.

Social Objective: Students will increase their poise and self-confidence.

Materials:
- make-up
- mirrors
- camera (i.e., Polaroid)
- cotton, etc.

Directions:
1. Divide the students into groups of four. Try to make sure that there is someone in each group who has made the most of their facial features, hair, and makeup.
2. Have each member of the group share the one or two facial features that they like about themselves. Then have each member tell every other member what feature they like best.
3. Pair students. Ask them to share with their partners the one thing that they would like to enhance or change about their appearance.
4. With cosmetics, as a team, students could come up with some ways to enhance each other's image and try them.
5. Get students to return to the group. See if they can identify the change and evaluate from a make-up point of view if they created the illusion they sought. This can be carried further to the whole face.

Time: One to two class periods

Notes to Teacher:
A. From our study, we found that attractiveness is a very important component of acceptance at the senior high level. Also, it has a tremendous effect on one's self-confidence.
B. Discussion on make-up should take place prior to doing this activity.
C. If approached from a theatrical, business-like manner, students can really enjoy this experience.
D. An outside speaker such as a clown, mime, or local make-up artist might be a wonderful addition to this activity.

BLIND DATE

Subject: Drama & Communications   **Grade Level:** Jr. & Sr. High

Content Objective: Students will become more aware of their talents and abilities in the field of dramatic performance. This activity can be adapted to encourage a monologue, dialogue, or soliloquy — whatever may be the instructional unit at hand.

Social Objective: Students will re-evaluate their attitudes and actions toward a possible blind date.

Materials:
- telephone — as a prop

Directions:
1. After studying what a monologue is, and experiencing some famous monologues, students will be asked to think about a given situation. They can do improvisation first. Afterwards, they can think about it in a more serious tone and present it on paper and/or orally to the class.

2. An example of a relevant monologue might be: A boy calls a new girl in class and asks her to a party. She has just met him and vice versa. What does he say? What might he be thinking? Remember that students will be doing a one-sided conversation (monologue).

Time: Two class periods

Notes to Teacher: Class discussion should cover the following topics of concern:
- Relating to others is a two-way street.
- Remember the Golden Rule and treat new acquaintances accordingly.
- There is much that takes place that affects people's feelings. Think about the repercussions of what you are saying. You are dealing with a person with feelings.
- Students should be encouraged to get to know all types of people.

UNDERSTANDING YOUR FEELINGS

Subject: Drama and Communications   **Grade Level:** Jr. & Sr. High

Content Objective: Students will identify feelings and act them out. They will become aware of their own feelings and how they communicate non-verbally.

Social Objective: Students will identify their feelings and the feelings of others.

Materials: • situation cards

Directions:
1. Students will be given situation cards to act out. The format of the lesson which should be explained to all students before they play charades is:

When _____, I feel _____.
              (a situation occurs)   (an emotion)

The students need to decode what the situation is that's causing the emotion and also what the emotion is.

For example:

When my parents are angry at me, I feel sad.
        (situation)   (emotion)

2. Choose from these situations or develop your own.
   a) Being grounded.
   b) Flunking a test.
   c) A favorite pet dying.
   d) Meeting someone who is handicapped.
   e) Being invited to a party.
   f) Taking care of younger brothers and sisters.
   g) Getting a good report card.
   h) Being new in your school.
   i) Not understanding the assignment.
   j) Getting your driver's license.
   k) Having your picture made.
   l) Eating a hot fudge sundae.
   m) Not getting a present for your birthday.
   n) Getting your hair cut.

Time: One class period

A RESPONSIBLE CITIZEN

Subject:	Social Science **Grade Level:** Jr. & Sr. High
Content Objective:	Students will develop a commitment to responsible citizenship by being well-informed in regard to their duties and responsibilities.
Social Objective:	Students will evaluate their own roles as citizens.
Materials:	• paper • pencil

Directions: Instruct students to do the following (use form below):

1. Fold paper in half. On one side, write down 10 attitudes or actions a responsible citizen should exhibit.

2. On the other side, do a self-evaluation checking those items that you presently do.

3. Pick one area that you do not presently do and would like to improve. Dividing into small groups, exchange ideas on specific steps to take for accomplishing your goal.

4. Develop an action plan or commitment in writing on how to make this change.

5. Get back together in a week or a month and share what you have accomplished.

Time: Two class periods or can be followed through in two weeks.

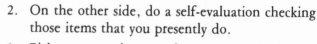
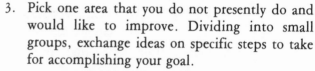
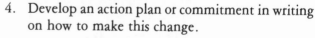
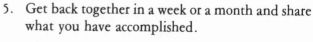

A RESPONSIBLE CITIZEN

BEING A RESPONSIBLE CITIZEN

Eight Important Characteristics of a Good Citizen	Characteristics That I Model and How
1.	
2.	
3.	
4.	
5.	
6.	
7.	
8.	

One area that I will be working toward is:

Steps that I will take to meet this goal are:

1) _____

2) _____

3) _____

What I have done this week toward my goal: _____

_____

_____

_____

Signature _____

RESOURCES IN YOUR COMMUNITY

Subject: Social Science   **Grade Level:** Senior High

Content Objective: Students will list and describe resources available to cope with mental health problems in a positive way for themselves, friends, and family.

Social Objective: Students will evaluate themselves and become aware of mental health problems. They will identify resources in their community where they can seek help.

Materials:
- list of agencies in community, e.g., State Mental Health Agencies, Alcoholics Anonymous, Drug Abuse Agencies, Psychologists, Psychiatrists, Therapists, Child Abuse etc.

Directions:
1. Give students a choice of problems to research. Have them work in teams of two (those interested in same topic).

2. Encourage students to visit a facility related to the topic of their choice. Ask them to do the following:

   a) On visitation, interview a person and find out what resources are available.

   b) Tour the facility.

   c) Obtain brochures, pamphlets, pictures, to use as handouts to class.

3. After visiting the facility have student pairs give a five-minute report to class orally on their agency.

4. Have students hand in a 5" x 8" index card providing the following information:

   a) Name of Agency   b) Address
   c) Phone Number   d) Contact Person
   e) General Resources Available
   f) Steps to follow if you need this resource for yourself
   g) Steps to follow if you need resource for a family member

Time: One to three weeks

Notes to Teacher:
A. Cards can be filed in class. They could be typed up and published for use by students, families and school. A copy should be in the school library and other places on campus where students might go for helpful information.

B. You may need to structure time for students so they know where and what they should be doing on the project in designated intervals.

FINDING MY ROOTS/
ARE WE RELATED?

Subject: Social Science   **Grade Level:** Jr. & Sr. High

**Content
Objective:** Students will identify and accept their ethnic and cultural heritage.

**Social
Objective:** Students will heighten self-awareness and self-concept.

Materials: • paper   • materials for display and portfolio

Directions: 1. A portfolio of family roots will be the outcome of this research project. Students will gather as much information as possible from the library, older family members, and other available resources. They may use interviewing techniques, notetaking, or other methods that you may want to encourage.

2. Pages within the portfolio can focus on:

a) Family tree — names back to great-great-grandparents.

b) Map of the world — trace family migration.

c) Something special about my family is...

d) Old photographs.

e) Chronology — interesting things about each individual in family, present, and past.

Time: A semester project

**Notes to
Teacher:** Students should be encouraged to bring in letters, Bibles, photographs, or other memorabilia that may have been passed through the generations in their family. A class bulletin board display and sharing time can be incorporated into weekly classes. A word to the wise: Be careful of sentimental, precious family items that cannot be replaced easily.

POEM ON HERITAGE

From many areas of Germany my ancestors came
Seeking their fortune, money, and fame.

In the late 1800's my ancestors arrived,
And in the beginning they barely survived.

But survive was the very thing they did.
They bought some land for a very low bid.

They started a family and a dairy farm, too;
Over lands in Wisconsin the sweet breezes blew.

With World War I the father had to leave.
That he would return they could only hope and believe.

He fought in dark and gloomy trenches,
Not able to sleep on anything, not even benches.

He lived with sickness, famine, and death,
But he struggled to breathe one last breath.

For years he remembered the green grass of home,
Yet he was without toothbrush, shaver, or comb.

After many years he finally returned.
His heart, now a cinder, still lovingly burned.

His children grew older, had kids of their own —
Who wore out the clothes their mother had sewn.

Their daughters, now teens, soon became courted.
And more immigrants were constantly being imported.

One daughter met a man and they got married.
And over the threshold his wife he carried.

The two of them moved to a lake called Pewaukee
Which is very close to the place of Milwaukee.

Suddenly World War II began...

The husband was drafted and soon went to war.
When the countries of the world at the Nazis were sore.

He fought on beach, cliff, mountain and plain,
Hoping his mind could keep from insane.

As his body was fatigued and his health grew worse,
Hitler and his Nazis he damned and cursed.

As a human being he willed not to die,
And to kill every Nazi that passed his eye.

He didn't think he was going to survive,
But his wife was ecstatic when he came home alive.

In that tiny house on that puny little lake
David Scheu was born and that's no mistake.

They moved to a house called Kavanaugh Place
Long before man thought of traveling in space.

At the age of 14, high school he faced
On the year many orbited around in space.

At eighteen he joined the Navy to sail the seven seas,
But for some reason in the winter all he did was sneeze.

At the end of his senior year he and Debbie met
They loved each other very much and the date was set.

They got married February 3rd, 1968;
They went to California; his ship left from that state.

Debbie then sailed to the Orient...

They lived there for about half a year.
Then David got orders to go somewhere near.

They had one more year to live away from the States,
But after all they were lifelong mates.

And on June 3rd, 1969, David Scheu, Jr. was
Made in Japan but all American parts —
German, English and Irish — well almost!

By David R. Scheu, Jr., Chula Vista, CA

I'M ALWAYS AN "A"
EVEN WHEN I DO "D" WORK

Subject: Social Science   **Grade Level:** Jr. & Sr. High

Content Objective: Students will gain a greater understanding of realistic expectations.

Social Objective: This activity will focus on students realizing that their self-concepts should not be tied in with the grades they receive. They are still okay when they've failed. It just means that they need to work harder or that the circumstances of the situation were out of their control.

Materials:
• pop quiz

Directions:

1. Give the class a pop quiz on something the students will *ALL* do a poor job on. Randomly give everyone a "D" or "F." Hand them back to your students. Notice their facial reactions as well as their behavioral changes such as frowning, acting out, and verbalizing negative comments about the test or teacher. Write these down.

2. After the initial shock, have your students write down how they felt and what they thought about themselves when they saw the grade.

3. Share your notes and their reactions. Have a group discussion about how a grade on a paper reflects their academic performance rather than their self-worth. The grade should indicate what they know and what they need to learn.

4. Also discuss what it's like to have others see when you've done a poor job.

Time: One class period

Notes to Teacher:

A. Another discussion could focus on understanding that we shouldn't always carry around the burden of "having to make an A on a paper." It's an unrealistic expectation.

B. Also, there could be a discussion relative to the "Normal Curve" as it relates to academic abilities. You might discuss the concept of grade inflation.

I'M ALWAYS AN "A"
EVEN WHEN I DO "D" WORK

C. Discuss the possible feelings of a hypothetical student who —
despite trying his hardest — was unable to make a good grade.
What are some alternatives for this student? This discussion should
be handled very carefully.

FEELINGS

Sometimes I think
I am useless!
Sometimes I think
that I'm not much at all.
But if God put me
on this earth,
I must be worth
something . . .
Just maybe even
a little something,
But at least that's better
than nothing at all.

By Lynette Figueras
San Diego, CA

PRODUCTIVE WAYS
TO COPE WITH STRESS

Subject: Social Science   **Grade Level:** Jr. & Sr. High

**Content
Objective:** Students will identify the causes and methods of coping with their own stress.

**Social
Objective:** Students will heighten self-awareness.

Materials: None

Directions: 1. Instruct students to research a technique from the following list. Feel free to add to this list in a class discussion:

    a) Nutrition
    b) Exercise
    c) Relaxation training
    d) Meditation
    e) Positive thinking
    f) Biofeedback
    g) Peer groups and support
    h) Healthy pastimes
    i) Ways to relieve anxieties/time management

    2. Small groups of students may work together to create displays to inform others of the benefits of various techniques.

    3. Students can share their research by putting on a "Be Good to Yourself Fair." They can invite other classes and parents to participate.

Time: Three to five weeks.

**Notes to
Teacher:** A. This activity is a good one to help foster good community relations.

    B. Guest speakers from the community can be used to enhance student research.

    C. If you have a stress test available, allow students to take it. Discuss how they can use this information to identify stressful elements in their environment and lives.

    D. You might invite the school nurse to class to show students how to measure heart rate and blood pressure. Discuss how these affect their level of health.

WHO ARE YOU?

Subject: Career Education **Grade Level:** Jr. & Sr. High

Content Objective: After completing this activity, students will be able to formulate and ask questions suitable for interviewing other persons with the purpose of getting to know them better.

Social Objective: Students will enhance their self-confidence by being the VIP in front of classmates.

Materials: • chart, butcher paper, pens, markers

Directions:
1. Students will contribute suitable questions for interviewing peers so they can get to know them better. Teacher will record these on the butcher paper.
2. Next, get the class to agree on a suitable list of questions to be used to interview every classmate.
3. Every day a different classmate will be interviewed. This person, who will be the VIP for the day, has the option of not answering some of the questions. VIP could be given certain privileges for that day.
4. After everyone has been interviewed, ask class to try to remember commonalities that were shared by three or more classmates.

Time: Half an hour

Notes to Teacher:
A. This activity is a good alternative to class introductions. It helps to integrate the content objective with the social objective at the onset of the school year. It is an excellent resource for teachers to get to know the strengths and interests of particular students.
B. Students may also interview the teacher. The teacher, by being first, helps provide a model for conducting other interviews.

WHAT'S MY LINE? (A)

Subject: Career Education   **Grade Level:** Jr. & Sr. High

Content Objective: Students will explore career alternatives. They will determine how others have explored professional opportunities available to them and made realistic career choices. They will learn to develop interview questions.

Social Objective: Students will become aware of their own interests and abilities while bolstering self-concepts.

Materials: • books for job interview   • library   • current articles

Directions: 1. Present students with a list of people to research who have managed to excel in their chosen fields despite tremendous obstacles. Each student will choose one personality from the following list. Teachers should add to this list as needed:

Obstacles	Famous People	Careers
Blind and deaf	Helen Keller	Writer, speaker
Eyesight poor (wore glasses)	Anne Sullivan	Tutored Helen Keller
Physically handicapped	Franklin D. Roosevelt	United States President
Blind	Stevie Wonder	Singer/Musician
Deaf	Beethoven	Composer/Musician
Physically handicapped	Itzhak Perlman	Musician
Learning disabled	Nelson Rockefeller	U.S. Vice President
Blind	Ray Charles	Singer/Musician
No arms	Bonnie Consolo	Homemaker

2. Teachers will just provide the person's name. Students need to answer the following questions about their selected person:
   a. What is your person's chosen field?
   b. What obstacles or hurdles did he or she have to overcome socially, emotionally, and/or physically?
   c. List at least ten pertinent facts about the individuals such as:
      a) when they lived   d) individuals who influenced them
      b) where they lived   e) other information you would in-
      c) life events   clude in a biographical sketch

3. Have students write ten questions they would use in an interview that would help them get to know this person.

4. Have students list five things they learned from the famous person that would help them gain and keep a meaningful job.

Time: Approximately two class periods

68

WHAT'S MY LINE? (B)

Subject: Career Education   **Grade Level:** Jr. & Sr. High

Content Objective: Students will explore career alternatives and develop self-confidence.

Social Objective: Students will become aware of their own interests and abilities.

Materials:
• chair in front of class

Directions: A student sitting in the chair assumes the identity of a book character, historical figure, or currently well-known personality who, despite tremendous obstacles, has managed to overcome and excel. (Personalities can be those previously studied in Part A of this activity or others identified by teacher and class.) Use people such as: Helen Keller, Anne Sullivan, Franklin D. Roosevelt, Stevie Wonder, and Itzak Perlman. The rest of the class is to ask interview questions developed individually. Each person gets a chance to ask one question. The object is to uncover the identity of the famous person. The interviewing will stop after 15 questions. Students will record their guesses on an index card and why they chose that person. Take a class poll and see who was chosen. The class might discuss why this person "made it" and how he/she overcame his/her handicap to succeed professionally.

Time: One to two class periods

Notes to Teacher: The class should be encouraged to talk about some of the limitations students may have when trying to be employed. Also discuss possible solutions.

MY RESUME:
A PICTURE OF THE POSITIVE ME

Subject: Career Education   **Grade Level:** Jr. & Sr. High

**Content
Objective:** Students will learn how to write a resume.

**Social
Objective:** Students will explore their personal strengths as well as their job skills and experiences.

Materials: • paper   • pencil   • resume form

Directions: Students will learn about the rationale and components included in writing a resume. Have students go through the following steps:

1. When they do *educational background,* focus on accomplishments, i.e., awards, special recognition at each time period, K-3, 4-6, 7-9, 10-12 grades. Ask them to try to come up with at least two things that were positive experiences at each level. Example:

    K-3 - class monitor/100% attendance
    4-6 - safety patrol/participant in school play
    7-9 - band leader/pep club/intramural sports star
    10-12 - honor roll/chess club, etc.

2. When they do the *work experience section,* ask them to focus on responsibilities that they've had in their lifetime. They can use home, school, paying jobs, and/or volunteer work. Once again, they are to list at least two positives per category. Examples:

    K-3 - care of family pet
           - dinner aide (set table, wash dishes)
    4-6 - selling Scout cookies/housekeeping
    7-9 - babysitting/yard care
    10-12 - gas station attendant/candy striper/tutor

3. For *Special Skills:* Ask students to reflect on characteristics that would be desirable to an employer and write down at least five traits or qualities valued.

    Example: punctual   friendly   organized
              courteous   neat appearance

4. *References:* Ask students to list three people who think they are great!

Time: One to two class periods

**Notes to
Teacher:** Reflect on the positives. This activity is a good introduction before having them do a *real* resume. They will also learn the components necessary for writing any resume.

A JOB FOR ME

Subject: Career Education   **Grade Level:** Jr. & Sr. High

Content Objective: Students will identify personal strengths that can be applied to a future career.

Social Objective: Students will identify their positive characteristics.

Materials:
- ditto or overhead transparency
- *Dictionary of Occupational Titles*

Directions: Have students complete the checklist below.

A. Find a person in the class who has one of the listed abilities and have them sign their name on the lefthand side of it.

B. Each student should try to identify four or five things that describe him/her.

C. Using this information, students should think of three jobs that might utilize their three best skills.

D. Students should check back with the classmates that signed their sheet and see if they have any of the same jobs.

E. Students will evaluate themselves in the righthand column using the following scale:

No ability = 1   Slight ability = 2   Maybe = 3   Good = 4   Excellent ability = 5

Name of Classmate Who Possesses These Skills   My Rating (1-5)

1. _____ athletic ability   ____
2. _____ overall academic performance   ____
3. _____ sense of humor   ____
4. _____ mathematical ability   ____
5. _____ attractive physical appearance   ____
6. _____ public relations skills   ____
7. _____ mechanical ability (use of hands)   ____
8. _____ musical   ____
9. _____ artistic   ____
10. _____ dramatic   ____
11. _____ reading   ____
12. _____ writing   ____
13. _____ thinking   ____
14. _____ scientific ability   ____

SIGN IN, PLEASE

Subject: Career Education

Grade Level: Jr. & Sr. High

Content Objective: This activity familiarizes students with desirable personality traits that would relate to almost any job.

Social Objective: Students will pinpoint their personality strengths.

Materials: • ditto sheet of suggested form

Directions:
1. When introducing this lesson on desirable personality traits for getting a job done, have students complete the following worksheet. Students will gather classmates' signatures in the slots provided beside the personality trait. No one person can sign more than two traits. The first one that fills up all their signature spots is the winner.

organized	_____	prompt	_____
enthusiastic	_____	able to accept	_____
self-confident	_____	criticism	
dependable	_____	cooperative	_____
flexible	_____	good listener	_____
well-groomed	_____	good speaker	_____
motivated	_____	follows directions	_____
respects rights &		stays on task	_____
property of others	_____	honest	_____
patient	_____	supportive of	
persistent	_____	others	_____
friendly	_____	diplomatic	_____
good at details	_____	thorough	_____
productive	_____	creative	_____
		consistent	_____

2. Using this activity as an introduction, go through some of the traits as vocabulary. Also discuss how these can be achieved. Discuss the kinds of traits needed on the job.
3. End the class on a positive note, and have all students stand in a circle and very quickly state in one word what personality trait they think is their most desirable. This activity will take five minutes and enables everybody to walk out feeling good about themselves.

SIGN IN, PLEASE

Time: One class period

Notes to Teacher: This is a really good warm-up activity for starting a unit on desirable work traits.

WHO AM I?

Who Am I?
Sometimes I am like a shadow,
hiding behind things, afraid to be seen.
At other times I'm bold and brave,
afraid of nothing.
But then there are times when
everything goes wrong and life
seems to be against me.
But the days in my life that count most
are when I feel there is nothing
I can't do!
That's when I know who I am.
I'm me and no one else.

By Laura Cavanaugh
San Diego, CA

TRANSITION

Subject:	Science **Grade Level:** Jr. & Sr. High
Content Objective:	Students will appreciate, develop, and become aware of the interrelationships existing within the human body.
Social Objective:	Students will become aware of ways to deal with changes in their bodies during puberty. This activity will enhance their self-confidence.
Materials:	• student journals

Directions:

1. In lecture format, the teacher should deliver the information as objectively as possible dealing with physiological changes in puberty. Most adolescents are going through these changes at approximately the same time.

2. Teacher can have students enter comments into their confidential journal twice a week. Once per week the class can convene in a circular type discussion (forum), bringing up general topics of importance to all such as:

   complexion changes   hair growth
   height/weight changes   sexuality
   vocal pitch changes

Time: Once per week for as long as deemed beneficial.

Notes to Teacher:

A. Specific structure for class discussion is advised taking these ideas into consideration:

   a) No more than one or two topics at any one meeting
   b) Serious — no laughing
   c) Discussions and journals shall be held confidential
   d) Everyone needs to be there, but a student has a right to pass on verbal comments

B. Check with district regulations on covering information relative to these topics.

PEP UP YOUR ENVIRONMENT

Subject: Science   **Grade Level:** Jr. & Sr. High

Content Objective: Students will identify ways their environment can affect their mental attitude. The effects of light and color will also be evaluated.

Social Objective: This activity is designed to enhance the self-concept/self-awareness of students.

Directions:
1. Students will do research on how colors affect people's behaviors and the effects of positive thinking.

2. Ask students to evaluate their bedrooms at home by using the following questions to guide their responses.
   a) Do you have a place you can call yours?
   b) If a stranger walked into your room and didn't know you, what could he tell about you from your environment?
   c) How does it make you feel?
   d) What colors are used in the decorating?
   e) Is your environment what you would like it to be?
   f) Are there some realistic changes that could be made?
   g) Are there posters in your room? Why did you choose those particular ones? Does it tell anything about you as a person?

3. After students evaluate their environment, the teacher could bring in some concrete ideas on helping students pep up their environment. Examples:
   a) sunshine through a window   d) posters
   b) plants   e) organizations
   c) paint walls   f) friends & pictures/ make collages

Time: One class period

Notes to Teacher:
A. This activity could be a large group discussion, etc. Students can research how people react to colors. They can read studies done by others as well as some surveying of classmates' reactions.

B. You might ask a guest speaker to come to class who can do color analysis for what shades of colors people should wear. This is very popular and quite interesting.

C. Paint stores, interior decorators, or the art teacher on campus might provide a good resource.

MY SCHOOL ENVIRONMENT

Subject: Science   **Grade Level:** Jr. & Sr. High

Content Objective: Students will analyze their school environment as it relates to their individual needs.

Social Objective: Activity will help students feel more positive about themselves and the place that they experience daily.

Materials: • inventory

Directions: Ask students to complete the following inventory. Afterward they are to pick at least one area they would like to improve. Students who have chosen the same areas might be grouped. Have them develop some realistic ideas for changing that aspect. Let them develop a plan of action. Reinforce the idea that they have options and opportunities to make positive changes in their lives and physical environments.

Please put a check mark (X) under one of the headings of *often, sometimes, never,* to indicate the way you feel about what your school has to offer you as a person.

My School Environment

Does your school offer:

	often	*sometimes*	*never*
a) classes that make you feel happy to be there?	___	___	___
b) the chance to use your talents?	___	___	___
c) the chance to develop new talents?	___	___	___
d) a chance to cooperate and work with other people?	___	___	___
e) to mix with people of all races and cultures?	___	___	___
f) to join social clubs (sororities, fraternities, pep clubs, etc.)?	___	___	___
g) to join interest groups?	___	___	___
h) vocational training?	___	___	___
i) an opportunity to succeed in something?	___	___	___
j) a place to be with friends?	___	___	___
k) a comfortable environment (i.e., temperature/lighting)?	___	___	___

MY SCHOOL ENVIRONMENT

l) a chance to interact positively with teachers?   _____   _____   _____

m) support from your teachers?   _____   _____   _____

n) activities that you enjoy after school hours?   _____   _____   _____

o) aid or help when you need it?

       academic   _____   _____   _____

       social   _____   _____   _____

       emotional   _____   _____   _____

Time: One class period

Notes to A. This inventory provides students with an avenue to explore their
Teacher: school environment and how they feel about it. Discussion and
             concrete suggestions for improvement might ensue.

           B. The inventory could be expanded to a five choice range if students
             can handle more variance.

           C. Students can add their own questions to the inventory.

           D. This information might be shared with the principal to give
             him/her some student feedback. Also teachers can use it to identify
             areas of needed improvement.

FACE UP TO IT

Subject: Science

Grade Level: Jr. & Sr. High

Content Objective: Students will develop skills to improve health, skin care, and dental hygiene.

Social Objective: Students will become more aware of their bodies and how to improve their assets. Improvement in self-concept will be realized.

Materials:
- toothpaste
- shampoos
- creams/soaps

Directions:

1. Ask everyone to bring in a box or label from their shampoo, toothpaste, and soap.

2. Make a group list of ingredients used for each product. Some of these chemical ingredients may need to be researched by students.

3. Have them compare common ingredients and then find out what those ingredients do to a person's skin.

4. Do some kind of analysis of what type of skin the students have. Help them identify the types of ingredients they should be using.

5. Have each student develop a skin care program to follow. Have them do a pre and post test to measure results of the program. One example of a pre/post evaluation might be taking a Polaroid picture before and after the skin care program. They can look for visible differences.

   A call or visit to a cosmologist at a local department store will provide the teacher with skin evaluation forms.

   Another option is to make up your own evaluation instrument as a class and duplicate enough copies so that each student will have two. Examples of areas to evaluate might be:

   a) dry areas of the face
   b) oily areas
   c) areas with acne
   d) coloring
   e) condition of hair

6. The skin care program should be followed for six weeks or more.

FACE UP TO IT

Time: One to two class periods/six week homework project

Notes to Teacher:

A. A cosmologist or dermatologist would be an excellent guest speaker.

B. Teachers should be careful about how they introduce and implement this lesson if there are students who have very sensitive health problems.

C. Special health problems may have to be referred to the School Nurse.

ME, MYSELF, AND I

There are many different sides of me
I'm sometimes quiet or rather shy
But sometimes I'm very bold.
I am a very special person in my own way
I can love with all my heart
and hurt with all my soul.
I can make a quest for my only dream
or I can reach for the highest star
I may be different, strange, or even weird
But I am a human being...I'm alive.

By Laura Cavanaugh
San Diego, CA

TARGETING

Subject: Science   **Grade Level:** Jr. & Sr. High

Content Objective: Students will identify problems, make observations, record data, interpret data, and make predictions based on their work.

Social Objective: Students will learn something new about themselves. They will develop their own self-improvement contract.

Materials: • chart   • worksheet   • notebook

Directions:

1. Students need to choose a habit or behavior that they would like to increase or decrease. This behavior should relate to improving and helping them become healthier, better persons, i.e., stop smoking, lose weight, increase physical fitness, say positive things, improve athletic ability, improve skin care routine, etc.
2. Ask students to observe this behavior for one week and record the following information: when it occurs, why it occurs (what triggers it?), with whom it occurs, how often does it occur? They are to keep a daily tally.
3. Have students determine a realistic goal for one month.
4. Have them determine how they are going to reward themselves.
5. All of this information should be recorded in a personal notebook.
6. Pair students in groups of 2-4 to act as a support system. They will help each other monitor their target behaviors.
7. Students will make out a contract based on their individual information and determining their goals.
8. Ask students to make a graph on a daily basis to report the frequency of behavior.
9. Have them analyze weekly in their notebook their progress and explain why they have (or have not) accomplished their goal. They should then predict their progress for the next week and make suggestions for going forward. This information should also be recorded in their notebook.
10. If the short term goal is accomplished, at the end of each week students should be rewarded by their support group, as well as enjoying previously determined tangible or social reinforcement such as: going on a date, going to the arcade, going to McDonald's, getting a special privilege from parents, going to a movie, or having a picnic.

Time: Five-ten minutes per day for a month

TARGETING

Contract Form

Name: _____

Target Behavior: _____

Classmates in my Support Group: _____

_____

_____

Specific things we plan on
doing to support each other: _____

_____

_____

My goal for this week is: _____

_____

_____

If I accomplish this goal: _____

_____

Weekly Record:	Comments: _____
Frequency of Target Behavior	_____
_____	_____
_____	_____

DANCING TO MY TUNE

Subject:	Physical Education	**Grade Level:** Jr. & Sr. High

Content Objective: Students will practice various types of dance routines.

Social Objective: Students will cooperate with peers as well as be in the limelight.

Materials:
- records or tapes
- record player or recorder
- mats
- costumes (if desired)

Directions: Gear some units specifically toward self-awareness.

Examples: Expressive dance   Vaudeville
Eastern type dances   Jazz
Karate, Judo

Have students pick out popular melody from an era. In pairs they can do a gymnastic type routine or dance. Planning the routine steps, practicing at home, and creating costumes should be fun as well as a learning experience. Students can perform for each other. Peer-evaluation or clapping can be used as feedback for the pair that planned and performed the routine.

Time: Homework project and three to four class periods to see everyone's routine.

Notes to Teacher: Many young women and men at junior high level enjoy practicing popular dances as well as making up their own steps and dances. If boys have a hard time, encourage gymnastic type routines.

GAMES

Subject: Physical Education   **Grade Level:** Jr. & Sr. High

Content Objective: Students will follow directions. This activity reinforces the rules to a particular game.

Social Objective: This activity will show the non-athletic students that they can enjoy and be good at a sport.

Materials:
- Electronic or boxed games relative to baseball, football, soccer, hockey, etc.

Directions: This lesson is a good rainy day activity or alternative to a paper and pencil test. Many students know the rules to the game in question but lack the gross or fine motor skills to play the game properly. The use of an electronic or boxed game to illustrate the rules of a game is multisensory as well as reinforcing. Have students work in pairs or small groups to avoid having particular students feel like "outcasts." Personal attention and positive socialization skills are encouraged in this situation. The destructive powers of a large group dissipate when students can have a positive experience with different peers on a small group or dyad basis.

Time: One class period

Notes to Teacher:
A. Students who do not have the gross motor skills to win on the field might be able to be winners in this situation.

B. This approach could be used as a reward for students who did well on an exam or met a goal in physical education.

C. Students can bring their own games from home and share them with the class.

LOOKING GOOD

Subject: Physical Education   **Grade Level:** Jr. & Sr. High

Content Objective: Students will self-evaluate their physical attributes and limitations. They will develop a program for physical self-improvement.

Social Objective: Students will enhance self-awareness.

Materials:
- tape measure
- form run off
- standard chart of measurements

Directions: Each student will be weighed and have their measurements taken by the teacher during the first week of school, if possible. Information such as listed in the box below will be recorded. You may wish to ditto this information as well as other pertinent data on a 5x8" index card for each student. This will make it look professional; similar to how records are kept at spas and commercial health clubs.

On Mondays, students will weigh and report their weight throughout the semester. Measurements will be taken monthly. Students and the teacher will observe changes in skin complexion and posture, as well as body weight. Use of a standard chart for measurements would be helpful to students when they determine their goals for improvement.

With a partner, have students discuss ways to achieve their goals. They will then develop an action plan on this exchange of ideas.

This is a good time to relate P.E. to attaining better physical conditions via nutrition, exercise, and positive attitude.

This chart should be maintained and self-monitored weekly. Students might keep food intake and exercise diaries as well as their card.

Students who achieve their goals should be given special recognition and an opportunity to share with others how they did it. This will provide a model for others as well as positive reinforcement for achieving students.

LOOKING GOOD

Here I Am	Healthy Ranges to Strive for	Areas I Need to Work on	Action Plan to Achieve Goals	Foods to Avoid
Weight _____	_____	_____	_____	_____
Arms _____	_____	_____	_____	_____
Legs _____	_____	_____	_____	_____
Chest _____	_____	_____	_____	_____
Waist _____	_____	_____	_____	_____
Hips _____	_____	_____	_____	_____
Comment on general posture:				
Skin/ complexion:				

Time: Ongoing throughout semester

Notes to Teacher:

A. Remember this can be a very sensitive area for students, especially overweight ones. Make sure you give extra support and reassurance to these individuals.

B. You might supply or set up a library of magazines and books that deal with diet, health, and exercise. It's important for the information to be accessible to students. Have them read related materials for homework. Students may also want to contribute articles they've found from newspapers and magazines.

WAYS TO REACT WHEN I LOSE

When I lose, I'm usually depressed, but after a while it rubs off. Sometimes when I lose it's not really fair, and I get really mad until I get my way or somebody calms me down. When other people lose, I try to cheer them up. I really don't like to lose, but somebody has to.

By Michelle Beyer, Chula Vista, CA

RUNNING FOR YOU

Subject: Physical Education   **Grade Level:** Jr. & Sr. High

Content Objective: Students will participate in cardiovascular exercise and attain a higher level of physical fitness.

Social Objective: Students will increase their proficiency in a sport and feel good about it.

Materials:
- track shoes
- place for running, measured and mapped out
- notebook for each student to keep record charts of performance

Directions: This program should be implemented at least three times per week, 10-20 minutes per period.

1. Obtain books, films, and speakers from the Heart Association. Ask for a representative to come out and talk to the group about the positive benefits of walking fast or jogging.

2. Next, discuss with students a realistic goal to work toward both as a group and individuals. (This will vary according to interests and abilities.)

3. 1st day — Everyone runs as far as they can. Have students time each other and keep track of distances. This information will be recorded in students' notebooks as a starting point.

4. Have students develop realistic four-week individualized plans.

5. Have students run three times per week around a pre-determined track.

6. Give students a choice of improving the distance they are running or the number of laps.

7. After four weeks, students should evaluate themselves and make a weekly plan for improvement.

8. Progress should be graphed by each student. The culminating activity could be to explore fun runs in the community that they could work towards entering as a class. Afterwards, a class picnic could be planned.

Time: Unit of study

RUNNING FOR YOU

Notes to Teacher:

A. 50- or 100-miler T-shirt might be a special incentive for students.

B. This activity should be viewed as an individual progress plan, not competition between students. It should be introduced and continued throughout the year. Students should be reinforced for encouraging one another. All progress should be evaluated in relationship to where the person started.

C. For those that cannot jog, the same system can be used for fast walking or wheelchair speed and endurance for the handicapped students.

D. You may wish to use stories such as the one about Glen Cunningham who was nearly burned to death as a child, but as an adult became America's fastest miler in the 1930's.

E. Avoid using jogging or running laps as a means of punishment for students. This will defeat the purpose of the program.

WHY BEING PHYSICALLY FIT IS IMPORTANT TO ME

I like being physically fit. It's fun exercising which is one thing I'm decently good at. It helps me look somewhat better and keeps me healthy. During the summer I always lose weight because my family goes camping and there's so much to do all day long. There's no time to eat, so I lose weight. I also get a nice tan and my hair gets blonder.

I also like to try to keep ahead of my friends in P.E. They're usually a little ahead of me in other subjects, so I try to make up for it in P.E. It's also fun because you just do sports and no bookwork.

I used to be rather pudgy until the 4th grade, and I didn't like sports. But then I started playing tackle football with the kids across the street, and I joined softball, so I am no longer pudgy.

By Jeanne Saville
Chula Vista, CA

JUNK FOOD JUNKIE

Subject: Physical Education   **Grade Level:** Senior High

Content Objective: Students will analyze and increase their energy level. They will identify factors that relate to being physically fit.

Social Objective: Students will enhance self-awareness.

Materials: None

Directions:

1. Have students keep a 14-day log of their own food intake, writing down all meals and between-meal snacks. At the end of each day, they should estimate caloric intake. During P.E. class, they should record energy level going into class and again at the end of the period. In addition, have them evaluate their own performance.

2. Discussion during this time should center around different nutrients and why they are important for good physical maintenance.

3. Lists of daily activities and calories needed per hour to participate can be distributed. Students can then subtract the calories they used from their daily intake to see if they are taking in the right amount and appropriate high protein foods rather than empty "junk food" calories.

4. Using this information and new knowledge, the students will try for two weeks to eat more high protein foods, foods with more nutritional value, foods without sugar and salt, and foods that have not been processed.

5. Students will then keep track of their energy level and their performance at P.E. daily.

6. Students should also note any changes relative to:
   a. Complexion   b. Skin color
   c. Alertness   d. Pep and gusto
   e. Temperament

7. Finally, have students compare week one with week two.

JUNK FOOD JUNKIE

Time: One unit of study — approximately 5 minutes per period.

**Notes to
Teacher:** You might make this a competitive project for mutual support. Reward those who comply with the rules. If you choose to make this competitive, use teams rather than individuals.

DREAMS

*The clouds slowly drift by, as I lie
under a tree shading me. The wind
gently blows across my face, while
I dream of my future; standing in
front of a class teaching children
with expanding minds; wearing a long,
white wedding gown, walking up an aisle
to meet the one I love. But I may not
last that long. Only God knows,
and I should live my life day by day,
instead of thinking of the future
or mourning over the past. I should
concentrate on today. Then my life
will mean more to me and others.*

*By Julie Sorgi
San Diego, CA*

GENERAL IDEAS FOR P. E. CLASS

Subject: Physical Education   **Grade Level:** Jr. & Sr. High

Social Objective: Self-awareness

Materials:
- P.E. fields and equipment
- a good role model
- a healthy attitude

Directions: The following are some general suggestions for P.E. teachers to follow to help enhance all students' self-concept while still dealing with the game content and competition of everyday classes.

1. Try to set up a system where students can choose some of the units of study. In racquet games, if given a choice between racquetball, tennis, or badminton, students can choose their course of study according to what they would enjoy more or achieve more success doing. Build in a self-evaluation section of the grade. Students can evaluate themselves according to specific criteria that you have previously set up. This helps students get a more realistic picture of their own strengths and weaknesses.

2. When charting skills, chart progress, and always reward improvement. Measure individuals as much as possible against themselves. An explanation of why they should do their best is important to discuss.

3. Stress to the students the importance of being a *good* spectator. One may not have the proper skills to play, but they can have an important role of rooting others on.

4. Create activities where students can compete against themselves. There are no winners or losers in this situation. If a student got three baskets last time, can he/she get four this time?

5. A buddy system may help in certain activities. Pair students together so that the strong person can help out the weaker one. A peer tutoring approach might be a good method to practice certain skills as long as your strong student has enough maturity and self-confidence so that he/she doesn't feel a need to show off or rub it in.

6. Choose teams according to something arbitrary such as colors of clothing or who had oatmeal for breakfast. This insures a good random mixture of abilities on each team. When this task is left to students, too many feelings are hurt.

7. Try to explain and model a healthy competitive spirit. Too often when one's team loses, the loss gets transferred to the individual member's self-concept. Talk about such concepts as: "let's try our best always"; "someone has to lose"; "we can't all be winners all the time."

8. Explore activities listed in *The New Games Book* edited by A. Fluegelman: The Headlands Press, Inc., 1976, or *The Cooperative Sports and Games Book* by T. Orlick, Pantheon Books, 1978.

9. Give a special award to students who put forth the most energy. This practice will emphasize that effort is as important in sports as the ability to perform at a high level of competence.

10. When planning activities, plan various activities to make different people shine. Let everyone be a captain. Give those who are not confident or competent the choice to have someone help them.

11. Set up a program where each team or class gets reinforced with a certain number of points for winning an event. Reward those who are good sports and exhibit good sportsmanship with points, also. This emphasizes the idea that, "It's not important if you win or lose but how you play the game." Explain on paper as well as orally what sportsmanship is and the types of behaviors that you will be looking for.

   For example:

   a. Sharing equipment
   b. Working with a new person
   c. No putdowns, just encouragement
   d. Shaking hands before and after a competition, etc.

   Then set up a chart in the locker room. Reward points at sporadic intervals according to when you see good sportsmanship. Remind the class daily which students received points and what they did to earn it.

   Promise the winning class at the end of the semester a special game, a field trip, or an Olympic Day.

   Follow through on individuals that have exhibited good sportsmanship with special recognition in the form of:

   a. Awards
   b. Captain for a day
   c. Special privileges to help the teacher, etc.

OPENING THE DOOR WIDER:

EXPLORING ONE'S OWN ATTITUDES, FEELINGS & ACTIONS

CHAPTER V

OPENING THE DOOR WIDER: EXAMINING ONE'S OWN ATTITUDES, FEELINGS, AND ACTIONS

Chapter V

Methods and strategies included in Chapter V provide opportunities for students to explore their feelings, attitudes, and actions toward those who seem unfamiliar or different. The goal is to look past the obvious differences (i.e., skin color, physical handicaps, etc.) and focus on the strengths and similarities of others. Lessons in this chapter emphasize the common theme: we all have limitations and weaknesses we strive to overcome, and that this practice is an acceptable part of life. In the meantime, we capitalize on our strengths and the positive attributes of others.

Many of the lessons encourage previously unfamiliar students to work together on a particular project. This temporary break-up of pre-existing friends is intended to find and develop newly-discovered commonalities between classmates. Working together in this indirect approach, while striving to attain a common goal, can become the impetus to opening further communication channels. The increased proximity and exposure between classmates provided in these lessons fosters cooperation and true empathy as opposed to pity and sympathy.

Attitudes and feelings are difficult to change — but possible. The authors of *Unlocking Doors to Self-Esteem* offer the lessons in Chapter V as one step in breaking down stereotypic barriers in regard to age, sex, handicaps, religion, race, and culture. A creative and accepting teacher, a positive social climate, and students possessing positive self-esteems are other important keys to "unlocking doors of friendship." These keys lead to opened communication channels, acceptance, and inclusion of all classmates.

BRAVE NEW WORLD

Subject: English   **Grade Level:** Senior High

Content Objective: Students will identify the plot, characters, and themes of an assigned novel.

Social Objective: Students will explore their attitudes, feelings and actions toward others.

Materials:
- paperback copy of *Brave New World* or another book with a similar theme.

Directions:

1. Have students read the book *Brave New World* by Aldous Huxley. Discuss themes of the book relative to one's position in society, i.e., alpha, beta, gamma, delta, etc.

2. Students should then try to empathize with the different designated sections of the Brave New World society. A written or oral discussion on what it would be like to be an alpha or delta, etc. should take place.

3. Another question to address is: Is there a way for us to change our position in our society?

Time: A unit of study

Notes to Teacher: Other books that lend themselves nicely to this discussion are:

     a) *Lord of the Flies* — Golding

     b) *1984* — Orwell

     c) *Catcher in the Rye* — Salinger

     d) *Soul on Ice* — Cleaver

     e) *Black Boy* — Wright

FACTS VS. OPINIONS

Subject: English   **Grade Level:** Senior High

Content Objective: Students will differentiate between statements which are facts and those which are opinions. They will analyze the views of editor on the editorial page.

Social Objective: Students will explore their own opinions. They will learn to present their opinions without turning other classmates off. They will also practice being persuasive in a positive manner.

Materials:
- paper
- pencil

Directions:

1. Give out some controversial topics relative to important aspects in your students' lives. Some examples are:

   a. Should we teach subject areas in two different languages?

   b. Should school athletes have good grades to get scholarships?

   c. Should special education students be in regular education classes?

   d. Should sex education be taught in schools?

   e. Should religion or the creation theory be taught in school?

   f. Is suspension or expulsion from school an effective way to deal with problem students?

2. Ask students to choose one of the following formats:

   a) Team up in groups of four. Ask them to come up with a consensus as an answer to the assigned question. Then ask them to write an editorial relative to their position. (This is a process activity as well as one in which students develop a product.)

   b) Give a persuasive speech to the class while taking a stand on an issue.

3. The goal of this lesson is to present their opinions without turning others off. Have a group discussion about this aspect of the assignment before they start.

FACTS VS. OPINIONS

4. Important points they should include are:

   a) There may be similarities in goals. What are some of the approaches to attaining them that are acceptable?

   b) Discuss that a view can be a personal one.

   c) Listen to another's opinion; try to identify a common ground.

   d) Avoid putting the other person on the defensive by being abusive or name calling.

   e) Remember everyone has a right to his/her own opinion.

   f) America was founded on four freedoms, one of which is freedom of speech.

Time: Two to three class periods.

Notes to Teacher:

A. A possible warm-up activity is to have students read editorials from a newspaper in class or as a homework assignment.

B. A panel of adults discussing a controversial topic might present their views to the class. These individuals could contribute ideas to a class discussion on the important points to include under #4 of Directions on this page.

C. A newspaper editor would be an excellent guest speaker.

CHILDHOOD MEMORIES

Subject: English   **Grade Level:** Jr. & Sr. High

Content Objective: Students will do a written composition incorporating proper grammatical components of written expression.

Social Objective: Students will explore their feelings about a problem common to themselves and others of a similar age. They will utilize problem-solving skills and attempt to resolve a dilemma.

Materials:
- construction paper
- colored pencils
- markers
- magazine pictures

Directions: Students will design a children's book about a problem that happened to them as a child. In order to do this they will first have to decide what will be included — this can be done by an outline. The conclusion of the story should present a resolution to the problem — either real or fictitious.

Time: Two class periods to one week.

Notes to Teacher:
A. This activity can also be implemented in groups as an oral discussion. Students who don't know each other well may come up with some commonalities of prior experiences.

B. The final product could be shared with younger students or made as a gift to parents or someone special.

MY GUINEA PIG DIED

My guinea pig died.
Should I or should I not cry?
It's not "only an animal."
They have feelings too.
They live, eat, breathe and drink
*   like all of us do.*
But I still don't know if I should cry.

By Julie Sorgi,
San Diego, CA

DARE TO BE DIFFERENT

Subject: English

Grade Level: Jr. & Sr. High

Content Objective: Students will draw meaningful conclusions from selected readings and relate them to their own experiences.

Social Objective: Students will explore their own attitudes, actions and feelings toward others.

Materials:
• paperback copies of *Jonathan Livingston Seagull* by Richard Bach.

Directions:
1. Have students read *Jonathan Livingston Seagull* for homework.
2. Discuss the story using the following questions:
   a) What do you think the moral of the story is?
   b) Should people always conform?
   c) Why do you think Jonathan had a need to be different?
   d) Do you think all seagulls look and act alike?
   e) Do you think all people of one race or culture look or act alike?
   f) Do you think all individuals with the same handicapping conditions look or act alike?
3. Develop additional questions that will aid them in generalizing the concepts of this study to things and experiences in their own lives.

Time: Homework and one class period

BUT I CAN

They say, "I can't run," but I can watch.
They say, "I can't talk," but I can listen.
They say, "I can't build," but I can plan.
They say, "I can't see," but I can imagine.
They say, "I can't read," but I can hear the stories.
They say I can't do much;
But I can move mountains
...if you help me.

By Tara Nicholson
Oceanside, CA

IT'S NOT FUNNY

Subject: English   **Grade Level:** Jr. & Sr. High

Content Objective: Students will be able to distinguish fact from opinion. They will become familiar with different sections of the newspaper.

Social Objective: Students will explore racial, political, and sexist prejudices presented in media.

Materials:
- clipping of cartoons from comic strips and editorial page of the newspaper, e.g., "Cathy," "Wee Pals," "Sally Forth," "Doonesbury," etc.

Directions:
1. Students will bring in a copy of the Sunday comics. If they don't have access to one, they can share. The ensuing discussion should revolve around what the comic strips say and the attitude and prejudices the author is trying to make the readers aware of.
2. Reactions can be written also.
3. Different groups of students should analyze different comic strips.
4. The class can keep a running bulletin board or scrapbook of these comic strips. These could be classified according to topic at hand, i.e., racism, sexism, handicapism, stereotypes, poking fun at public figures, political figures, etc.

Time: One class period or ongoing unit done weekly

Notes to Teacher:
A. Discussing the enjoyment students get from reading comics and funnies in the newspaper can highlight another common pastime of classmates.
B. It's important to get across to your students that there are often hidden meanings or social statements presented in the comic strips they read.

KELLY

Friendly, patient, kind, and understanding

Sister to Bret

Loves to swim, ride her bike and read

Who feels left out because she can't run

Who feels happy because she can swim

*Who feels loved because she has friends
    who care about her*

Who fears having an accident with her wheelchair

*Who fears people will not accept her
    because she's crippled*

Who fears going to the doctors

Who would like to see herself walk

*Who would like to be able to do things that
    normal, healthy children can do.*

*Who would like to see nothing but the best
    come to her family.*

Kelly was born with a disease called Osteogenesis Imperfecta which means her bones can't grow the way our bones grow. Yet she tries hard to do the things that we do. Kelly is a real super woman.

By Paul Northeimer
San Diego, CA

A NEW CLASSMATE

Subject: Drama and Communications   **Grade Level:** Jr. & Sr. High

Content Objective: Students will develop the ability to work in a spirit of cooperation within a group. They will solve problems involving time factors in order to complete a given task.

Social Objective: Students will be forced to look past the obvious. They will explore attitudes, feelings and actions toward those who are different.

Materials:
- situation cards
- props if needed or desired

Directions: 1. Divide students into groups of four or five. Give them one of the following situation cards. Give them five minutes to plan their presentation *without any teacher explanation or expectations.* Students will then role play the situation in front of the class.

Suggested Situation Cards to Role Play:

I am an eighth grader. Reading has always been difficult for me. I don't like school much and I fool around in class a lot. Sometimes the teacher hassles me and the whole class is watching, so I act like it's just a big joke. I really feel dumb and I hate school.

I am a diabetic. I look just like you do and I can do everything that you guys can. My body has a hard time processing sugar properly. I am not supposed to eat sweet, sugary things such as soda, ice cream, candy, and cakes. If I do, it can be very bad for me.

A NEW CLASSMATE

This female student practices a religion that believes that dancing and wearing slacks are sins. The class has just earned some money and one idea is to have a special western dance just for the 7th grade.

I just got admitted to a regular PE class in school. This is a big thing for me, because a few years ago I was in a car accident and lost my right arm. That was really hard because I used to be the star of my little league. Well, now they are picking teams for a class intramural competition. I wonder if anyone is going to choose me?

2. A class discussion should take place revolving around the following questions: How would the new classmates feel? What are some alternatives for coping with the situation?

3. Students should then be given the opportunity to reenact the skit. (Expect students to overprotect and nurture the student this time.)

4. A third try should be given. This will show the complete cycle students will go through.

Time: Two to three periods (One to two periods role-playing, one period for discussion)

Notes to Teacher: Most likely the students will progress through three stages when doing this activity: rejection, oversympathy, and finally appropriate treatment.

OUTER SELF

Subject: Drama and Communications   **Grade Level:** Jr. & Sr. High

Content Objective: Students will do a self-evaluation, and receive feedback from others. They will discuss how their moods affect their means of dress.

Social Objective: Students will explore their own attitudes, feelings, and actions toward themselves and others.

Materials:
- checklist (form attached)

Directions:

1. Students will enter class and take five minutes to reflect upon their day. They will write how they felt when they got up this morning. This is a personal exercise and will not be shared with others.

2. Students will then jot down what they are wearing that day and how they feel about each item that they have on.

3. Questions to provoke thoughts and discussions are:

   a. Is there a relationship between what you have on today and how you felt this morning?

   b. What are you saying to others in your choice of clothes today?

   c. How are others seeing you?

4. Students will interview five other students of their choice and ask them, "Judging from the clothes I have on, what kind of mood do you think I'm in? Am I representing myself the best way I can? Any suggestions? A sample of an anonymous checklist that students may use has been included below:

   a. Where is it appropriate to wear what _____ is wearing? school _____, church _____, ballgame _____, date _____, work _____, home _____, other_____.

   b. What mood do you think he/she was in when dressing this morning?

   c. Give two suggestions for improvement.

Time: One to two class periods

OUTER SELF

A. Depending on your students' maturity level, you may wish to preface this activity with a projection type exercise using characters from an existing script. Plays that may be relevant are:

- *The Put-Down Pro*
- *The Big Hassle*

by Jack Canario,
Janus Book Publishers,
Hayward, CA

Discuss the characters in the play in terms of their attitudes, personalities, how they see themselves, and how others see them. Further discuss what kinds of clothes would project their attitudes and perceptions.

B. A TV program that will facilitate the social and academic objectives of this lesson might be "The Facts of Life." Then discuss in class how each character dresses and how their choice of dress reflects their feelings about themselves and the image they are projecting to others.

LEARNING FROM THE MEDIA

Subject: Drama and Communications   **Grade Level:** Jr. & Sr. High

Content Objective: Students will develop an appreciation and understanding of drama, including its background, history, acting principles, and production techniques.

Students will develop an interest in dramatic literature and dramatic performance as a part of their cultural lifestyle.

Social Objective: Students will explore their own attitudes, feelings, and actions toward those who are different.

Materials: None

Directions:
1. Teachers and students should be encouraged or required to view contemporary local and national theatrical productions, movies, and TV performances dealing with the following themes:

Films Dealing with Handicapping Conditions

All God's Children	signing/deaf
Butterflies are Free	blind
A Patch of Blue	blind
Coming Home	physical
A Day in the Life of Bonnie Consolo	physical
Circle of Children	emotional
Sunrise	autism
Sybil	emotional
Three Faces of Eve	emotional
If You Could See What I Hear	blind
Who Are the Debolts?	multihandicapped
Elephant Man	physical
Miracle Worker	blind/deaf

Films Dealing With Cultural Differences

Zoot Suit
West Side Story
Fiddler on the Roof
My Fair Lady
Roots
Guess Who's Coming to Dinner?
To Sir, With Love
Chariots of Fire

Films Dealing with Aging

On Golden Pond
Tribute
Sunshine Boys
Going in Style

Films Dealing with Sex Differences

Nine to Five
Kramer vs. Kramer
Unmarried Woman

2. Class discussion should ensue.

LEARNING FROM THE MEDIA

Time: A unit of study

Notes to   A. Field trips can be taken.

Teacher: B. One of these stories could be used in a class production for the year.

C. Students could be required to write a review for the school newspaper or class newsletter.

D. Check local afternoon TV listings. Sometimes there are some good older films that would be applicable.

FOCUS ON THE POSITIVES
OF OTHERS

Subject: Drama and Communications   **Grade Level:** Jr. & Sr. High

Content Objective: Students will experience the development and writing of a skit. Given a certain situation, students will take an idea and express it on paper — formulating a five-minute skit.

Social Objective: Students will focus on each other's positive strengths. They will explore their own attitudes, feelings, and actions toward those who appear to be different.

Materials: • cards   • envelopes

Directions:
1. Begin this lesson with a discussion on stereotypes — relative to age, handicaps, culture, sex, and race. Discuss the fact that stereotypes can be positive or negative. Get some students to share their experiences and feelings with the class in a non-threatening environment.

2. Next, divide the class into small groups of 3 to 4 students.

3. Then give each group an envelope with an index card in it. The card has one theme that they need to focus on. Possible themes are: sex, age, race, handicap of any type.

4. Given that card, the group will brainstorm with each other all the positive things that they can think of when dealing with the particular population.

5. Students will then write a skit that will demonstrate popular positive attitudes about their assigned population. This can be done as a group assignment and will take one to two class periods.

6. Scripts should be read, evaluated, and given feedback by teacher prior to a class presentation. This procedure will guarantee that only the positive attributes are presented in the skits.

7. Students present their skits. Peers will list and comment on the positives that may have surfaced in their classmates' skits.

8. A culminating discussion on stereotypes can take place with a focus on looking at the strengths of each individual rather than constantly trying to put them into a group.

FOCUS ON THE POSITIVES
OF OTHERS

Time: Four to five class periods including preparation time. Prep time and writing the skit can be incorporated into a group project or homework assignment.

Notes to Teacher: Stereotypes are a part of life. Focusing on the positive ones and downplaying the negative ones can be a beginning to breaking down some barriers between students.

CINQUAIN

Lonely People
Insecure, unaccepted
Waiting, aging, dying.
All they have is their faith and hope
The Wasted.

The Physically Handicapped
Different, "Not Normal"
Trying, hoping, succeeding
A sign of hope and inspiration
Unbreakable Spirit.

By Alex Bleza
San Diego, CA

109

WHAT ARE WE *REALLY* SAYING?

Subject: Drama and Communication   **Grade Level:** Jr. & Sr. High

Content Objective: Students will realize the effect that a performance (media) has on the audience or observer. They will pinpoint what is being communicated.

Social Objective: Students will become aware of what various forms of media are promoting in their commercials dealing with stereotypes, individual roles, etc.

Materials: • opaque projector

Directions:

1. The goals of this lesson are to have students interpret advertising techniques used by the advertiser in magazines, TV, newspapers, and other forms of mass media.

   To facilitate this, teacher should bring in examples from magazines of advertisements depicting one of the following populations in a negative light — also some in a positive or changing light (handicapped, female, young person, old person, black, Chicano, etc.). A discussion revolving around the following questions should introduce this lesson.

   a) What is being shown? (What are they advertising?)
   b) How do you feel seeing it?
   c) What is the advertisement really saying?

2. Give students a homework assignment to look through any available magazines, newspapers, comic strips, etc. They are to choose an example — one positive and one negative — to share with the class on the opaque projector. They are to think about why they chose those pictures and explain their conceptions to their classmates. Students can also hand in a short, one-page synopsis for the teacher.

3. After they have done this activity, students can start to observe what is going on in their own lives — the kinds of input they are getting from other forms of media — TV, plays, radio, etc. What are these mediums really representing? What types of stereotypes are they perpetuating? Are there any changes taking place?

Time: Two to three class periods

Notes to Teacher: This is a good activity to introduce students to another form of media — the opaque projector.

HANDICAPS DON'T HAVE TO BE LIMITING

Subject: Social Science   **Grade Level:** Jr. & Sr. High

Content Objective: Students will identify contributions of different members of society.

Social Objective: Students will realize that they all have disabilities and that many can be overcome.

Materials:
- guest speaker — someone who has an obvious physical handicap, but leads a productive life in spite of the disability.

Directions:

1. Invite a guest speaker who has a handicap to talk to the class. Have the guest speaker tell about using strengths to overcome weaknesses and limitations.

2. On the following day have a class discussion focusing on the fact that everyone has disabilities although many are not as obvious as those of the guest speaker.

3. Students will then evaluate themselves as to their strengths and limitations in these four areas: emotional, social, physical, and educational.

4. They will then list two strengths and two weaknesses in each area.

5. They will note a way to improve each weakness as a homework assignment.

Time: Two to three class periods

Notes to Teacher:

A. A list of resources or places students may go that are available to aid them in accomplishing their goals may be provided.

B. Ask the special educator in your schools to provide you with a list of guest speakers in your area.

PEOPLE IN THE NEWS

Subject: Social Science   **Grade Level:** Senior High

**Content
Objective:** Students will summarize current events orally or in writing.

**Social
Objective:** Students will explore their attitudes, feelings, and actions toward others focusing on the positive, i.e., what an individual *can* do.

Materials: • bulletin board   • newspaper articles   • magazine articles

Directions: 1. For a month prior to this activity, students should collect articles from magazines and newspapers dealing with people overcoming weaknesses or challenges. This will create a general classroom awareness and appreciation.

Examples: a) an individual with a handicapping condition overcoming or compensating for his handicap, b) efforts of minorities (racial, cultural) to attain equality in an adverse situation.

2. Students will collect five different articles on same theme (a or b) and summarize them orally or in writing. An oral evaluation may lend itself to better peer discussion and integration of the social objective.

Time: One month

WHY I'M PROUD TO BE AN AMERICAN

I am an American! In those few words I express freedom, love, free agency, freedom of speech, and so much more. In these few words I show ideals that people have fought and lived for and others have fought and died for.

America is the country I love. We are not under a dictatorship or monarchy. Our government is a democracy so we choose our leaders and we speak our minds. We live lives of freedom and opportunity.

This was made possible by people who had dreams of freedom. They made those dreams into goals, and those goals became America. Be proud to say "I am an American," for you are.

By Amber Callahan, Chula Vista, CA

TAKING A STAND

Subject: Social Science   **Grade Level:** Senior High

Content Objective: Students will familiarize themselves with their citizen responsibilities. They will gain knowledge of their democratic rights and freedoms. They will analyze current federal, state and local problems.

Social Objective: Students will gain a greater understanding of their attitudes, feelings and actions toward individuals with handicaps. They will gain awareness of political issues that directly affect them or their classmates.

Materials:
- paper and pencil
- library
- copies of laws relative to topics of interest

Directions:
1. Have students research one of the following topics or any others that involve discriminatory practices:

   a) Job discrimination relative to hiring the handicapped.

   b) Integration of special education students into the regular class.

   c) Provisions of differential standards for graduation for Special Education students.

2. Encourage them to take a stand on the issue. Have students write their Congressman/woman relative to their opinions.

Time: One to two weeks

Notes to Teacher:
A. A class debate might be an interesting enrichment project.

B. The entire class may wish to give support for a specific bill going through the legislative process. Discuss how to go about getting involved and try it.

ROLLING TO WIN

Subject: Social Science   **Grade Level:** Jr. & Sr. High

Content Objective: Students will develop an empirical approach toward thinking and respect the opinions of others who, through the same process, have reached different conclusions.

Social Objective: Students will explore their attitudes, feelings, and actions toward others.

Materials: • one die

Directions: 1. Students will participate in a discussion to answer the following question: If they were given three wishes, what would they be?

2. Representatives from the class will be called upon to roll the die. Depending on the number rolled, students will take the role of one of the following:

   a) If students roll a 1, then they will take the role of an adopted child whose real parents are dead.

   b) If students roll a 2, then they will take the role of a student who is blind.

   c) If students roll a 3, then they will take the role of a Vietnamese refugee.

   d) If a 4 is rolled: a student who is mentally retarded.

   e) If a 5 is rolled: a very rich child.

   f) If a 6 is rolled: an 80-year-old person.

   Students will then try to empathize with the situation called for and discuss how their wishes would change if they found themselves in one of the six categories.

Time: One to two class periods

Notes to Teacher: Role keys can be changed according to pertinent subject of interest to the class, i.e., historical or geographical aspects of people living in their community.

STEREOTYPES

Subject:	Social Science **Grade Level:** Jr. & Sr. High
Content Objective:	Students will begin valuing attitudes and behavior that enable men to relate to each other as human beings, rather than as stereotyped images.
Social Objective:	Students will focus on physical cultural characteristics.
Materials:	• butcher paper or blackboard • markers
Directions:	1. Students will break into small workable groups (No more than five).
	2. Teacher will provide a list of five cultures and/or races represented in their geographical location or discussed in a student text.
	3. Students will brainstorm and list stereotypes they have about each culture/race. They can tape their group lists in proper culture category on the chalkboard or on butcher paper.
	The class will then compare lists and see which things appear most often.
	4. A class discussion of stereotypes and prejudices that everyone has can ensue. Now students will be asked to identify someone they know who doesn't fit the stereotype.
	5. Concepts for discussion include:
	a) Stereotypes perpetuate negative connotations.
	b) Stereotypes affect a person's individual self-concept.
	c) Our goal is to look past traditional stereotypes.
	d) Gut reactions and group discussion should be encouraged.
Time:	One to two class periods
Notes to Teacher:	A. One way to get students to internalize this subject matter is to have them anonymously write their gut reactions. Have them tell what stereotypes they think people put them in and how they feel about it.
	B. This activity can be modified to deal with handicap stereotypes, successful person stereotypes, ethnic, or minority stereotypes.

GETTING ALONG

Subject: Career Education   **Grade Level:** Jr. & Sr. High

Content Objective: Students will identify communication skills needed to get along with co-workers.

Social Objective: Students will explore their own attitudes, feelings, and actions toward others.

Materials:
- situation cards

Directions:
1. Put students in dyads. Give each pair a situation in which there is a disagreement between co-workers.

    EXAMPLES:

    a. Worker A doesn't believe that co-worker B has done his share of the work.

    b. Worker A thinks co-worker B took credit for something he (A) did.

    c. Co-workers A and B are competing for the same promotion.

    d. Worker A was chosen to take a trip that co-worker B wanted to take.

3. Have them solve the problem in a positive manner. Compromising may be necessary by both parties.

4. As a class, allow pairs to share their solutions. Since other classmates will be analyzing the same situation, have them compare their approaches. Discuss the importance of getting along with others on the job.

Time: One to two class periods

Notes to Teacher: An entire lesson can be done on effective communication techniques. Thomas Gordon has excellent books that provide specific strategies that can be taught to your students.

WHO'S QUALIFIED?

Subject: Career Education   **Grade Level:** Senior High

Content Objective: Students will develop an awareness of others' qualifications. Students will also become familiar with the major laws that govern employment.

Social Objective: Students will explore their attitudes, feelings, and actions.

Materials: • paper   • pencils

Directions:
1. As an introduction to this lesson, have students do a homework project in which they do a library search on laws that govern hiring practices in their state. Have each student focus on information pertaining to one of the following areas:
   a. Sex
   b. Handicapped persons
   c. Race
   d. Age

2. As a class, have students discuss discriminating hiring practices.
   a. Why are these practices perpetuated?
   b. Why was there a need to have laws governing these practices?
   c. Are these laws ever abused by the employees?
   d. What recourse do you have if this happens to you for one of the above reasons?

Time: Homework assignment and one class period

Notes to Teacher: There is an excellent video-tape or film called *A Different Approach* that would be beneficial to show and discuss. The tape can be ordered from:

> South Bay Mayor's Committee
> for Employment of the Handicapped
> 2409 North Sepulveda
> Manhattan Beach, CA 90266
> (213) 545-4596

GET THE JOB DONE (Part 1)

Subject: Career Education

Grade Level: Jr. & Sr. High

Content Objective: Students will explore different career options relative to the skills required for specific positions. They will practice interviewing techniques.

Social Objective: Students will familiarize themselves with how to relate to possible employers.

Materials: • paper   • pencil

Directions:

1. Have students search their neighborhood for a place of employment (grocery store, secretarial services, xerox place, etc.). Ask them to choose one type of position within that establishment. Have them interview a representative of that position to find out what it is that they do. The following list will direct their questioning:

   Specific Questions for Students to Ask

   a) What is your job description?

   b) What specific skills are needed? (e.g., personality traits/tasks required)

   c) What in your background helped you attain the present position?

   d) What advice would you give someone who is interested in this profession?

2. Ask students to complete a form similar to the one below when interviewing:

   a. Place of employment _____
      Person interviewed _____
      Job title _____
      Work hours _____
      Transportation used to get to work _____
      Any benefits provided for transportation _____
      Hourly wage _____
      Rest breaks provided on the job _____
      Benefits such as insurance, etc. _____

   b. Please comment on the following:
      elevators   steps required   height of counters
      ramps   access to restroom   entrance to building
      existence of railings   availability of food

Time: Half of a class period to explain assignment. Homework assignment.

GET THE JOB DONE (Part 2)

Subject: Career Education   **Grade Level:** Jr. or Sr. High

Content Objective: Students will explore different careeer options relative to the skills required for various positions.

Social Objective: Students will explore some positive actions and modifications that can be made to accommodate a person with a particular limitation.

Materials: • index cards

Directions:
1. Students should come back to class with the prescribed information requested in part one. Each student will then choose an index card provided with an identity to assume written on it. They will then analyze the pros and cons of this individual taking a job in the place that they have researched.

2. After they have analyzed the pros and cons, they should list 3 realistic accommodations that could be done to enable this person to work in the environment studied. Examples for index cards:
   a. a female who is paralyzed and uses a wheelchair
   b. a male, age 40, who doesn't have use of his right hand
   c. a man, 68, who walks with a cane
   d. a woman who is 7 months pregnant
   e. a diabetic
   f. someone who has asthma
   g. a 16-year-old school dropout
   h. someone who only knows one language and it's not English

3. A group discussion should occur after students have made their decisions and recommendations. Listed below are some concepts that should be brought out.
   a. People shouldn't be denied a job because of a characteristic or trait that they possess, especially ones that they don't have too much control over.
   b. Some accommodations are easy and should be encouraged.
   c. Not every job is for everyone.
   d. One must have realistic expectations for oneself when looking for a job.

Time: Two to three class periods

The Inside, The True Person

By Paul Kreul
San Diego, CA

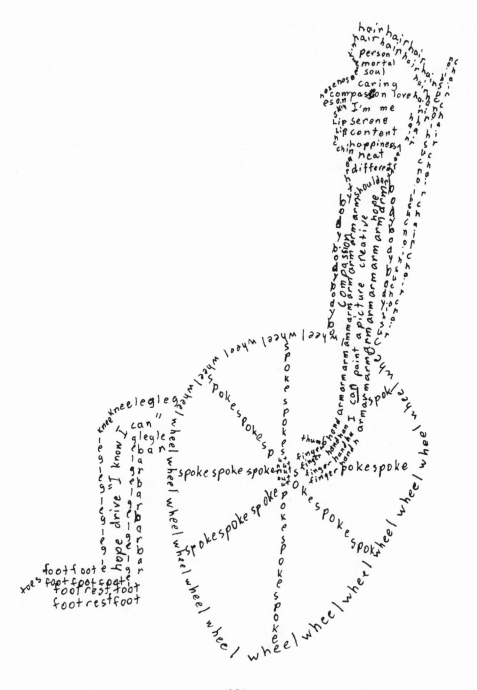

OPTIMISM VS. PESSIMISM

Subject: Career Education   **Grade Level:** Jr. & Sr. High

Content Objective: Students will acknowledge the importance of positive attitudes in getting and keeping a job.

Social Objective: Students will discuss how attitudes affect one's behavior. They will explore their own attitudes and feelings toward self and others.

Directions:

1. Have all students define the terms "positive attitude" and "negative attitude" on a piece of paper and give an example of both.

2. Have a class discussion about how important it is to have a positive attitude toward getting a job and keeping it. Discuss the self-fulfilling prophecy as it relates to self and others.

3. Teacher will make the following list on the chalkboard:

   a. the boss   d. the workplace
   b. hours   e. salary
   c. co-workers

   (List can be expanded from discussion.)

4. Students will arrange desks in a circle. Each student will then have to create a negative statement dealing with an assigned topic from above. Five students will take topic one, five topic two, etc., so that all students have a chance to verbalize a negative attitude about one aspect relative to getting or keeping a job.

5. Next, students will look at the same statement they made and revise it so that they verbalize a positive attitude.

6. Discuss the following concepts:

   a) How did you feel making the negative statement?

   b) How did you feel hearing all the negative comments?

   c) Do you think having a positive attitude about yourself and others would help you get a job? Or keep a job? Why?

   d) How does what we say affect what we do?

   e) How can we help our co-workers who complain look at things a bit more positively?

   f) What can you do as an individual not to perpetuate negative attitudes?

Time: One to two class periods

CRITICISM CAN BE HELPFUL

Subject: Career Education   **Grade Level:** Jr. & Sr. High

Content Objective: Students will discuss ways to accept and utilize criticism to their advantage.

Social Objective: Students will explore their own attitudes, feelings, and actions toward themselves and others, i.e., school, job, peers.

Materials: • ditto with story situations

Directions: 1. The following situations are given as a warm-up activity to begin this lesson. These situations can be put on the blackboard or on a ditto. Each student needs to read the situation and react to it on paper. No prompting from the teacher is needed at this point.

   a. **School**
   Roberta knows that part of her grade in social science is going to be based on oral class participation and attendance. She usually sits in the back of the room and just listens. Half way through the grading period the teacher indicates she has not been doing her job and that Roberta is expected to answer more oral questions.

   b. **Job**
   Miguel is working as a cashier at the local 24-hour market. Many of his friends stop by to patronize the store. However, the boss criticizes him for not giving the correct change and blames it on his socializing with the customers rather than paying attention to his job.

   c. **Classmates**
   Evangela tells Sue Ellen that she overheard the teacher say that her friend Amanda was going to fail the course if she did not make at least 80% on the next test. Evangela tells Sue Ellen not to tell Amanda. Sue Ellen tells Amanda so that she'll study. Evangela finds out and criticizes Sue Ellen for having a "big mouth' and "not being able to keep a secret."

CRITICISM CAN BE HELPFUL

2. After students have reacted to the situations, a class discussion should ensue. Make sure the class discusses possible steps to follow when they receive criticism. Some possibilities are listed below:

   a. Listen to everything the person is saying. Stay calm and open-minded. Avoid interrupting. Don't feel you have to reply right away.

   b. Think about what was said and how it was said. Determine what the objective of the criticizer was. Was he angry? Jealous? Trying to be helpful? Doing his job, etc.?

   c. What can you do or say that will help you deal with the problem appropriately? Students need to brainstorm some ideas. Examples:

      • Ignore the problem — it's not your problem.

      • Communicate with the criticizer some options so that you can correct problem.

      • Be assertive to criticizers. Let them know why you made your decisions. Be firm.

3. After discussing each situation, have students turn their papers over and resolve situations in a more appropriate manner.

Time: One to two class periods

USING AND ABUSING

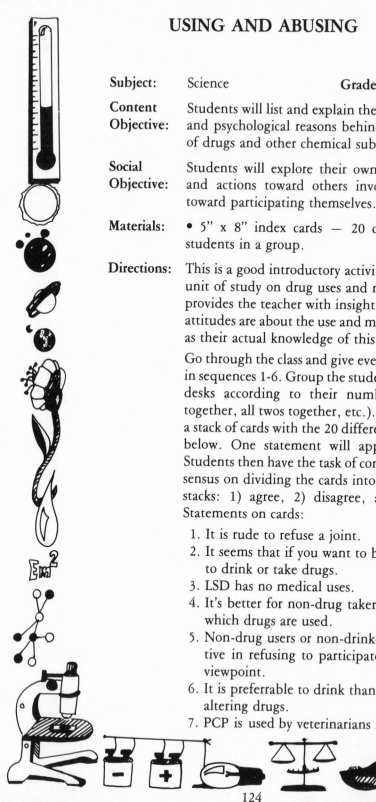

Subject: Science   **Grade Level:** Jr. & Sr. High

Content Objective: Students will list and explain the physiological effects and psychological reasons behind the use and abuse of drugs and other chemical substances.

Social Objective: Students will explore their own attitudes, feelings, and actions toward others involved in drugs and toward participating themselves.

Materials: • 5" x 8" index cards — 20 cards per group/5-6 students in a group.

Directions: This is a good introductory activity when beginning a unit of study on drug uses and misuses. The activity provides the teacher with insight as to what students' attitudes are about the use and misuse of drugs as well as their actual knowledge of this topic.

Go through the class and give every student a number in sequences 1-6. Group the students around tables or desks according to their number (e.g., all ones together, all twos together, etc.). Each group receives a stack of cards with the 20 different statements listed below. One statement will appear on each card. Students then have the task of coming to a group consensus on dividing the cards into the following three stacks: 1) agree, 2) disagree, and 3) undecided. Statements on cards:

1. It is rude to refuse a joint.
2. It seems that if you want to be popular you have to drink or take drugs.
3. LSD has no medical uses.
4. It's better for non-drug takers to leave parties at which drugs are used.
5. Non-drug users or non-drinkers should be assertive in refusing to participate and explain their viewpoint.
6. It is preferrable to drink than to use other mind-altering drugs.
7. PCP is used by veterinarians in treating animals.

8. Cocaine is addictive.
9. Sugar can be considered a drug.
10. When people are "high" they are a lot of fun.
11. Smoking pot gives you a sore throat.
12. After smoking one marijuana cigarette, it is safe to drive.
13. Getting high and getting drunk are different experiences.
14. Most drinkers feel a little uncomfortable with non-drinkers at a party.
15. You can't change a drug user or a drinker unless they want to give it up.
16. Fifty percent of the fatalities in auto accidents are substance abuse related.
17. One out of five youths (ages 14-17) who drink are problem drinkers.
18. Marijuana promotes a physical dependence.
19. If you are with someone who is on a "bad trip" you should call their parents first.
20. Mixing drugs and alcohol gives you a better "high."

Time: One to two class periods

Notes to Teacher:
A. This procedure enables students to explore their own ideas, feelings, and misconceptions which inevitably will be shared with others in the group. Also, students will see what their peers actually know and don't know about drugs. You can make up your own questions and play the game again at the end of the unit of study.

B. Guidance Associates has some excellent filmstrips and cassettes in the area of drug education:
- "Marijuana: Facts, Myths and Decisions"
- "Drug Information"
- "High on Life"
- "Me, Myself, and Drugs"

"NEVER"

Some of the most wonderful stories to read are about the "never" children.

The child the doctors say will "never" walk, who runs a marathon.

The child doctors say will "never" speak, who sings majestically.

The child doctors say will "never" be able to use his hands, who writes masterpieces or plays the piano with force ... yet gentle smoothness.

But what about those who don't have any special gifts? Maybe they are running and swimming and playing ... on the inside.

By Cynthia Rainbolt
San Diego, CA

UNDERSTANDING OUR BODIES

Subject:	Science

Grade Level: Jr. & Sr. High

Content Objective: Students will identify different parts of their anatomy, especially those relating to their respiratory system, digestive tract, and brain function.

Social Objective: Students will develop a positive attitude towards others. They will identify handicapping conditions in a positive manner.

Materials:
- textbook
- brochures
- speakers from community agencies
- films

Directions:

1. When students are studying the parts of the body and how they work, make sure they also study the handicapping conditions that exist when a part malfunctions.

2. In a discussion, bring out the incidence rate of each condition. Also discuss why these conditions are not diseases that happen to others but occur randomly within a large population.

3. Bring in speakers from American Diabetes Association, Epilepsy Foundation of America, United Cerebral Palsy Assn. or any other agency that deals with the handicapping condition being studied. They can provide movies, pamphlets, and other information.

4. Ask them to share information on preventative emergency procedures and what to do if someone has a problem in or out of the classroom.

Time: One to two class periods.

Notes to Teacher: Contact a special educator to get a list of local agencies that provide speakers, brochures and/or films on any handicapping condition you might wish to discuss with your students.

WHAT IT'S LIKE
TO BE HANDICAPPED

Subject: Science   **Grade Level:** Jr. & Sr. High

Content Objective: Students will identify how different parts of their body work and don't work. Particular emphasis will be on their eyes, ears, throat, and voice.

Social Objective: Students will foster positive attitudes toward individuals who are blind, deaf or hard of hearing, or who have speech and/or language problems.

Materials:
- blindfolds (enough for six students)
- cotton balls (two per classmate)

Directions:

1. When the class is studying the eyes, ears, throat and voice, bring in the concept of problems that might affect their performance.

2. Divide the class into three groups. Have each student pair up with one other person within their assigned group. Groups will rotate to each of the following activities:

   a) What it's like to be blind.

   b) What it's like to be deaf or hard of hearing.

   c) What it's like to have trouble speaking or using language.

3. Set up learning centers in your classroom. At each station students will do the following:

   a) *What it's like to be blind.* Have one partner wear a blindfold while the other partner leads him/her around the room. The blindfolded partner will do the following activities with guidance from his sighted partner: 1) write his/her name on the chalkboard; 2) pick up his/her books; 3) open the door; 4) get a drink of water; 5) walk up and down steps. Then the partners change places.

   b. *What it's like to be deaf or hard of hearing.* Have one student put cotton in his/her ears. The other student will say a sentence very quietly without looking at the person. See if he/she can guess what was said. Next time have them communicate something they want without using words (e.g., hand gestures, head movement, lip movement). Have students exchange tasks.

   c. *What it's like to have trouble speaking.* Have one partner read something from the textbook with his tongue touching the roof of his mouth. Can the partner understand? Exchange places.

WHAT IT'S LIKE
TO BE HANDICAPPED

4. After all students have experienced what it's like to have these handicaps, have a group discussion dealing with the following ideas:

   a. How did they feel?

   b. Would learning be harder for them if they had these handicaps?

   c. What are the aids, appliances, or machines that could help these individuals compensate for their loss?

   d. What are possible causes of each handicapping condition?

Time: Two to four class periods

A BALANCED MEAL

Subject: Science   **Grade Level:** Jr. & Sr. High

Content Objective: Students will familiarize themselves with the basic food groups and components of sound nutrition.

Social Objective: Students will explore their own attitudes, feelings, and actions relative to other cultures.

Materials:
- cookbooks from different cultures
- magazines such as *Sunset, Southern Living, Good Housekeeping,* etc.

Directions:
1. Students will divide into groups of four or five. Each group will take a different culture.

2. Students will apply the information they learn about nutrition in their science book to the choice of menus for their culture. Some background research may be necessary prior to beginning this lesson.

3. Students will look through their books and magazines and come up with a daily menu for their culture. They will then identify which food group each food item belongs to.

4. Discussion and nutritional evaluation should follow emphasizing different methods to achieve good balanced nutrition.

Time: Two class periods or a homework activity

Notes to Teacher:
A. Students should be grouped randomly so that members of the particular cultures being studied are dispersed throughout the class. This will familiarize students with something new to them and will help them examine their attitudes toward others.

B. Students can cook one item on their menu to share with classmates.

C. This activity can be one small part of a larger "Culture Fair" to be held in conjunction with Social Science and English Departments.

D. An interesting bulletin board of foods and cultures lends itself to this activity.

FROM SCIENCE TO DAILY LIVING

Subject: Science

Grade Level: Jr. & Sr. High

Content Objective: Students will relate the scientific method to problem solving in real life situations.

Social Objective: Students will explore their own attitudes, feelings, and actions toward others. They will become more objective before drawing conclusions about relationships. They will be able to support their attitudes with objective data.

Directions:
1. Introduce the steps involved in doing an experiment, i.e., "the scientific method to solving a problem."

    a. Problem
    b. Hypothesis
    c. Experiment — exploration
    d. Observation
    e. Conclusion

    Now relate these steps to *Problem Solving* strategies used in real-life daily situations:

    a. Identify the problem.
    b. Generate all possible solutions.
    c. Evaluate each solution.
    d. Decide on one solution to follow.
    e. Implement the solution.
    f. Evaluate its effectiveness.

2. Lead a discussion which will help students see that the scientific method is valuable in their daily lives as well as in the "lab." In the discussion focus on: a) the differences between opinions and facts, b) the importance of open-mindedness, and c) the need to look at numerous options before coming to a conclusion or making a final decision.

3. Some examples that could be discussed in detail to reinforce the new skills are:

    a. Prejudices reinforced by family
    b. Barriers to widening your opportunities
    c. Risk taking
    d. Broadening friendship circles

Time: One to two class periods

Let It All Out

By Michael Moeller
San Diego, CA

FLOOR TO MY KNEE

All my life I could not see
Anything from the floor to my knee.

There is nothing there.
I say, "I don't care."

But it hurts inside.
I'm very brave; I won't hide;

I can't run, or walk, or jump, or play
But I swear to myself I will one day.

By Tara Nicholson
Oceanside, CA

MIX-UP

Subject: Physical Education   **Grade Level:** Jr. & Sr. High

Content Objective: Students will participate in current unit team game such as: soccer, basketball, football, field hockey, or softball.

Social Objective: Students will experience not being the best in something. Students will gain an awareness of feelings for the person that's not very athletic.

Materials:
- equipment needed to play the chosen sport

Directions:
1. The object of this lesson is to have students play the position they play the worst, i.e., if you have a good pitcher, put him in an outfield position that he would have a hard time doing well. Suggestions for selection of positions follows:

   a. Draw a position from a hat.

   b. If teacher knows students' abilities well, then the teacher could assign them to a position that isn't optimal.

   c. Have students write their name and positions they prefer to play. Then when assigning positions, make sure not to allow them to play any positions they listed.

2. During the game, the teacher should make notes and grade students for their poor performance.

3. A class discussion should follow focusing on the following questions:

   a. How would you feel being graded on something you don't feel is a strength?

   b. Was your interest in this game as high as in a game where you're playing your strongest position?

   c. Did your teammates treat you any differently today?

   d. Do you know anyone who might feel like this all the time? Don't tell us who.

   e. How do you think they feel?

MIX-UP

f. How do you treat them?

g. What could you do as a teammate to help this person to feel more comfortable in physical education class? Examples that might be considered are:

- Practice with the person

- Focus on positives. Cheer others on and ignore it when they make a mistake.

- No yelling to make the person more nervous — give encouragement to your classmates.

- Switch positions. Don't focus as much on winning or losing but how the game was played.

Time: One class period

Notes to Teacher: For students who are good at all positions, have them use their non-dominant hand to play the game.

WAYS TO REACT WHEN YOU LOSE

Ways to react when I lose are to stay calm, not talk to anyone, and most of all to stay away from people. When I lose, my dad says I'm one of the poorest losers he has ever seen.

I think I'm a poor loser because of my striving to be better than my opponent. If I'm beat I think that I could have done better with myself. It makes me feel like I'm "no good" or that anybody can just come along, play better than me, and beat me.

In basketball when I play I do the best I can because it is personal pride for me to be better than the other person. During the games I run until it hurts to breathe; I take people on defense who aren't my assignments. I raise my teammates' spirits so they will play better and want to win. The reason I do this is simple. If the other people on the team see me working as hard as I can and making the team feel as though it is important to win, they will try harder themselves to win. "If I do win, then I don't have to worry about how to react when I lose."

By Greg Matthews
Chula Vista, CA

LOSING DOESN'T MEAN
YOU ARE A "LOSER"

Subject:	Physical Education	**Grade Level:** Jr. & Sr. High

Content Objective: Students will learn the rules of the game and the rules of good sportsmanship.

Social Objective: This activity fosters positive interactions with all people involved in the sport — not just the student's team.

Materials: • butcher paper   • tape   • markers

Directions: 1. Each time a new game is introduced to the class, the rules of good sportsmanship should be covered concurrently with the rules of the game.

   a) How to play
   b) How to win
   c) How to lose

   Brainstorming is a good technique for developing a class set of rules for good sportsmanship behavior for any game; e.g., in baseball you don't throw the bat; shake the hand of the person closest to you who is a member of the opposing team and thank him/her for a good game; and separate the game from your own personal worth.

Time: 15-20 minutes

Notes to Teacher:
A. Students would benefit from keeping an ongoing binder with rules of games and good sportsmanship-like behavior.

B. Many students in physical education classes would benefit from more structure. By covering the rules of sportsmanship along with the rules of the game each time a new game is introduced, these students know what is expected of them. Students with poor social skills need this information repeated and modeled by others.

C. Ditto rules of the game and sportsmanship-like behaviors pertinent to the game at hand. Give each student a copy to study. Test either orally or use a written exam. Post a copy on the bulletin board.

WHAT WOULD HAPPEN IF...

Subject: Physical Education   **Grade Level:** Jr. & Sr. High

Content Objective: Students will understand the challenges and frustrations of individuals who have physical limitations.

Social Objective: Students will explore their own attitudes, feelings, and actions toward others with handicaps.

Materials:
- rank order slips
- cottonballs
- wooden rulers
- tape for braces
- slings or handties
- blindfolds
- chairs or wheelchairs

Directions:
1. Have students prioritize how important the following things are to them: a) the ability to see; b) the ability to hear; c) the ability to walk; d) the ability to talk; and e) the ability to use their hands.

2. Relate each ability to the chosen game they are playing for the day. What would happen if they didn't have their most important ability? Give them a chance to experience this during PE class. Each student will participate the entire period without this ability. Use materials listed above to help simulate the handicapping conditions.

3. After experiencing this, students can answer the following questions orally:

   a. What kind of special considerations would you like to have had made for you?
   b. How did you feel about yourself?
   c. How did other classmates treat you?
   d. Why do you think we did this?
   e. What did you learn?

Time: One class period

Notes to Teacher:
A. It might be easier to concentrate on one handicap at a time. A fourth of the class could play the game with that disability. Time for a class discussion is *strongly* suggested.

B. *Handicapped...How Does It Feel?* packets for secondary level published by B.L. Winch & Associates can be used to help students simulate handicapping conditions.

HANDICAPS THAT I HAVE

Handicaps that I have are the handicaps of most people around my age. My biggest handicap is the video game craze. There are many others. I give in too easily. I sometimes put things off until later. When I'm mad I sometimes take it out on somebody.

I'm sometimes lazy. When I'm watching TV and my mom asks me to do a job, I slowly get up, nag, and do other things so I don't have to do what she asks. I used to have a TV handicap, but now I'm older I don't watch as much TV as I used to when I was younger. I also write too small and sometimes I am greedy.

Another handicap I have is that I sweat too, too much. I also have a habit of talking too much everywhere. I can't stay still for five minutes anywhere, especially when I am sitting. These are some of the handicaps that I have.

By Steve Noriega
Chula Vista, CA

SCAVENGER HUNT

Subject: Physical Education   **Grade Level:** Jr. & Sr. High

Content Objective: Students will get acquainted with classmates.

Social Objective: Students will identify classmates' strengths. They will get to know classmates and their commonalities. This activity shows that everyone is involved in sports in one manner or another.

Materials: • pencils   • ditto of list

Directions: Give students the following list or develop a similar one. Have students find classmates who can sign their names by a phrase or word that represents them in Physical Education. No one person can sign a list twice; however, they can sign the same item on numerous lists:

1. Knows the rules of football _____

2. Can dance _____

3. Has a good "serve" _____

4. A good scorekeeper _____

5. Loves to watch sports _____

6. Likes buttered popcorn _____

7. Knows the name of five outstanding women in sports

   _____

8. Takes shower every day _____

9. Has jacket, sweater, or T-shirt with school name on it

   _____

10. Plays on a school team _____

11. Watches Monday Night Football _____

12. Watches Saturday World of Sports _____

SCAVENGER HUNT

13. Jogs _____

14. Likes to camp out _____

15. Has competed in a sport contest or race _____

16. Goes to all school games _____

17. Would like to be a cheerleader _____

18. Is or has been in the school band _____

19. Tries his/her best _____

20. Is over 5 feet tall _____

21. Shows good sportsmanship behavior _____

22. Is a good fan _____

23. Can stand on his/her head _____

24. Can do a cartwheel _____

25. Collects baseball cards _____

26. Has baseball cap from an out-of-state team _____

27. Can name five different types of balls _____ ____

28. Has been boating _____

29. Can swim _____

Time: 20 minutes

LIMITATIONS

Subject: Physical Education   **Grade Level:** Jr. & Sr. High

Content Objective: Student will practice skills for the current unit of study (e.g., softball, volleyball, soccer). Student will follow good sportsmanship practices.

Social Objective: Student will experience how it feels to be limited in movement. They will identify coping skills they utilized.

Materials:
- equipment for game

Directions:
1. Class will play team game such as baseball, hockey, soccer, volleyball, or basketball.

2. Before the game begins, 3-5 people on each team will draw an index card from the teacher's hand that will describe their limitation for the first half of the game. For the second half of the game, students will pick a teammate to take over their limitation.

   Limitations might be as follows:

   a. Tie shoelace with a teammate's shoelace (i.e., work as a pair throughout).
   b. Hop throughout the game.
   c. Do NOT use dominant hand while playing.
   d. Be second to touch the ball or don't touch it at all.
   e. Always pass the ball to a teammate.
   f. Clap your hands before you touch the ball.

3. Debrief activity ten minutes before the end of the period. Use these questions:

   a. How did you feel having such a limitation?
   b. Did you develop a method to cope with your limitation and still be an active member of the team?
   c. How could teammates help you participate? Would "rooting you on" help?
   d. Why do you think the class did this activity?

Time: One class period

Notes to Teacher: Good resource for more ideas: *The New Games Book* edited by Andrew Fluegelman, Garden City, New York: Doubleday & Co., Inc., 1976, A Headlands Press Book.

KEEPING THE DOOR OPEN:

DEVELOPING POSITIVE RELATIONSHIPS WITH OTHERS

CHAPTER VI

KEEPING THE DOOR OPEN: FOSTERING POSITIVE RELATIONSHIPS WITH OTHERS

Chapter VI

Chapter VI is designed to provide secondary teachers with numerous "easy-to-do" motivating activities designed to facilitate their students' building of positive social interaction skills. This chapter furnishes teachers with a set of important lessons that focus on two major needs of the adolescent: a) becoming accepted by their peers, and b) developing effective communication skills to encourage widening their circle of friends. These lessons provide an abundance of opportunities for students to explore alternatives and consequences within a safe environment. Furthermore, the activities help to direct exploration (in a subtle way) toward encouraging development of appropriate and acceptable social skills.

Students are taught the necessary elements for building positive relationships, especially friendships. They learn to evaluate their own communication skills and discover ways to improve problem areas. For example, they begin to realize how important their body language and image are in how others perceive them.

Another essential skill they learn in their endeavor to widen their circle of friends is how to interact and feel comfortable with individuals who are handicapped, are of a different race, culture, age, religion and/or sex. Models as well as non-threatening opportunities are provided to help students deal with these social situations in such a way they personally grow from the interaction and involvement. Although they learn to focus on the commonalities rather than differences in the initial relationship, they do recognize and appreciate the individual differences that exist.

The thirty lessons included in this chapter have been field tested by secondary teachers from numerous classes. Each lesson has been evaluated as significant in aiding students in acomplishing their goal of being accepted while at the same time enlarging their own circle of friends. They also learn that both goals are attainable and can be handled in a socially appropriate and acceptable manner.

SAY IT WITH SCULPTURE

Subject: English, Art   **Grade Level:** Junior High

Content Objective: Students will be able to communicate a quality or idea by creating a sculpture conceptualization of an abstract idea.

Social Objective: Students will identify the elements of friendship that they feel are important and to compare these elements with what their peers see as important.

Materials:
- wire
- clay
- assorted junk such as string, material scraps, buttons, paper, etc.

Directions:
1. Students will use assorted junk to illustrate through sculpture some of the common elements of friendship. Examples of some modern art may be used to provide students with a jumping off point. Examples of some of these elements are:

   a) mutual trust   d) enjoyment
   b) compassion   e) communication
   c) cooperation   f) sharing

2. After the structures are completed, allow students to discuss elements they illustrated and explain why they chose them.

3. Further discuss the importance of friendships and ways to enrich as well as expand relationships with classmates.

Time: One to two class periods or as a homework assignment

Notes to Teacher: The socially isolated student will benefit from a class discussion revolving around the important elements of a friendship. Many of these students do not understand these elements and therefore have trouble applying them to social situations. Input from peers will indirectly aid in providing an appropriate model.

IMAGES

Subject: English   **Grade Level:** Jr. & Sr. High

**Content
Objective:**   Students will identify the plot and theme of a story or book. They will conceptualize and relate the theme to situations that may affect their lives or the lives of others.

**Social
Objective:**   Students will explore their attitudes, feelings, and actions toward others.

Materials: • books   • markers   • construction paper

Directions: 1.   Divide students into groups of four or six. Each member of the group will read the same book. There will be four or five different books covered in each class.

2.   You can use books from your required reading lists or choose books dealing with different struggles of the handicapped or minority individuals. You may wish to refer to Chapter Seven of *Unlocking Doors to Self-Esteem.* An annotated bibliography of young adult fiction relating to these topics has been included. A partial list is below:

   a. *But I'm Ready to Go* by Louise Albert.

   b. *Nancy and Her Johnny-O* by Bianca Bradbury.

   c. *You're Somebody Special on a Horse* by Fern Brown.

   d. *Stranded* by Matthew Christopher.

   e. *Shadow in the Sun* by Bernice Grohskopf.

   f. *Listen for the Fig Tree* by Sharon Bell Mathis.

   g. *Lisa, Bright and Dark* by John Neufeld.

   h. *The Cougar* by Martle Quimby.

   i. *The Lionhearted* by Harriet May Savitz.

   j. *The Cay* by Theodore Taylor.

3.   Once they've read the books, each student will develop five symbols that would represent significant themes of the book.

IMAGES

4. Groups will meet and discuss the various conceptualizations of each of its members. As a group they come up with a consensus of 4 to 6 symbols that would pictorially and conceptually represent common themes of the book. Using these components, they will do two things:

   a) Design a book cover to share with the class that represents the book's themes. (Use on bulletin board.)

   b) Do a group oral report to the class on their book.

Time: One week of class periods plus reading time.

Notes to A. Short stories, magazine, or newspaper articles could be used in
Teacher: place of a book.

   B. All students could read the same novel. Directions would be adjusted accordingly.

   C. Use of logos from various organizations and/or companies could be put on transparencies and displayed to students to help explain how to illustrate a concept.

POETIC GREETINGS

Subject: English   **Grade Level:** Junior High

Content Objective: Students will relate the meaning of poetry to their own experience.

Social Objective: Students will create and edit own writings to effectively apply creative and communicative skills.

Materials:
- pencil
- paper
- typing paper (folded in quarters)

Directions:
1. Students will fold typing paper in quarters. Students will decorate greeting card on the outside using the theme of friendship.

2. Students will create the poetic message on the inside for delivery to a classmate. This individual will be selected by a drawing. This insures that everyone will receive a greeting card.

3. Teacher should set the stage in a positive note. Greetings should only be positive. A class discussion revolving around the use of greeting cards should take place. Some questions to consider are:

   a. Why do you send a greeting card in the first place?

   b. How do you feel when you receive a greeting card?

   c. How would you feel if you received one that wasn't positive?

Time: One class period

Notes to Teacher: This activity can be implemented during certain times of the year such as: Valentine's Day, birthdays, Christmas. It also could be done for students who are out of school for a prolonged period of time because of illness.

LET ME INTRODUCE MYSELF

Subject: English   **Grade Level:** Jr. & Sr. High

Content Objective: Students will improve their skills in sentence structure, paragraphing, and using the appropriate letter writing formats.

Social Objective: An opportunity will be provided to present positive information about oneself to another. Consequently, students will widen their circle of relationships and open the door to communication.

Materials: • paper   • pencil

Directions:
1. Put all the names of students in a jar or box. Have students draw the name of somebody they don't know well.

2. Utilizing the correct format for friendly letters, have them introduce themselves and request information about the other person. If you choose, you can encourage a running communication.

Options that might be tried are:

a) Choose a different student each week.

b) Add some mystery to the task by having students not divulge their identity and then have students try to guess who wrote them.

Time: One class period

Notes to Teacher: This lesson might be followed by contrasting friendly letters and business letters.

IT'S A FRIEND

She's always there when I need her.
We share our thoughts.
I can trust her, because she trusts me.
We are very close even when we're apart.
We have serious talks
And have a lot of fun together.
We like the same things;
We hate the same things.
Can you guess? It's a friend?

By Tara Nicholson, Oceanside, CA

RECIPE FOR FRIENDSHIP

Subject: English   **Grade Level:** Junior High

Content Objective: Students will do creative writing and paragraph formation.

Social Objective: Students will be encouraged to think about the elements of friendship.

Materials: • 5" x 8" index cards

Directions:
1. Ask students to list at least five ingredients they feel are important for a good friendship to occur.

   Example ingredients:
   a) common interests
   b) mutual respect
   c) sense of humor
   d) loyalty
   e) athletic ability

2. Ask students to write a recipe for developing a good friendship using their own ingredients.

   Example: *Directions for Building a Friendship:*
   Mix 3 drops of humor to a relationship.
   Add common interests one at a time until well blended.

3. Every day the teacher can read one recipe to the class for thought provoking purposes.

Time: One class period

Notes to Teacher:
A. This idea might make an attractive bulletin board. Cut out or draw pictures of people walking hand-in-hand, smiling, of friends, etc.

B. This activity is a good one to provide models for those students in class who lack the proper social skills.

RECIPE FOR FRIENDSHIP

5 Cups of friendliness
3 Cups of care
3 Cups of love
4 Cups of dependability
6 Cups of trustworthiness
3 Cups of goodness
1/2 Cup of disagreement

Double the recipe, add another person and blend well. Set in the sunlight for days, then pop in the oven. When removed from the oven it will spring back and open, releasing a beautiful friendship.

Although not a food, the above ingredients are needed to make a good friendship.

By Steven Gregory
Chula Vista, CA

RECIPE FOR FRIENDSHIP

2 honest people
1 strong bind
    several good times
2 big, open hearts

Take the two honest people and create several good times with them. Stick the two big, open hearts together and tie them to make one strong bond. If you follow these directions it will never spoil. Whatever you do, *don't destroy*.

By Michelle Beyer
Chula Vista, CA

WHAT MY FRIEND IS LIKE

My friend is funny (funnier than I!) And we insult each other. Not to hurt, not to cry, not to do and die, but simply to tease. We got in trouble once before, and it seems we'll keep getting in trouble.

If I have a reason (which I don't) I'll use my friend as a model for this recipe:

> *One (1) full-grown, friendly person*
> *(1) person to use as other friend*

Take these two people, mix in pot, take glue and glue them together. (If they are good friends, they might always be together. Think about it!) Boil in love, companionship, arguments, humor, etc. Place in same neighborhood if convenient.

This friend may not conform to the friend stereotype (nervous, smiling hee-hee-hee) but at least a friend!

By Jonathan Rimorin
Chula Vista, CA

SPEAKING UP

Subject:	Drama/Communication **Grade Lev.:** Jr. & Sr. High
Content Objective:	Students will prepare an outline for giving a speech.
Social Objective:	This activity provides students with a peer model for dealing with social situations.
Materials:	• 3 x 5 index cards • visual aids of student's choice

Directions:

1. Students will choose one of the following topics. Teachers need to limit sign-up to facilitate an even distribution relative to the number of class members and topics.

   a. How to make a friend.

   b. How to meet a new person at a party.

   c. How to treat the new person in class.

   d. How to ask the teacher a question about an assignment that you didn't understand.

   e. How to join an already existing friendship circle.

2. Each student will make an outline of steps that one needs to know in presenting their "How To" topic.

3. Students will proofread the steps and then transfer their outline onto note cards. They can also develop visual aids such as overhead transparencies to use in their presentation.

4. Students will then give a how-to-do-it speech to the class.

5. Classmates will give fellow students feedback by writing down one thing they thought the presenting student did well and one suggestion for improvement.

Time: Two to four class periods

CLOSE ENCOUNTERS

Subject: Drama and Communication

Grade Level: Senior High

Content Objective: Students will learn to evaluate their own and others' performances in an objective manner. They will increase their ability to give both formal and informal presentations. Students will acquire increased poise and self-confidence in group acting situations.

Social Objective: The activity will provide students with a model of how to act around an individual of the opposite sex.

Materials: • role cards with situations.

Directions:

1. Teacher will divide class into six groups. The groups will act out one of the following situations. A discussion and input will be done after each role play. A second group will re-enact the situation with the suggested modifications. This format will be followed until all three situations have been performed.

   a. Girl meets boy or vice versa in a pizza place after school. She knows him from her math class. She thinks he is attractive.

   b. You are at a school dance. You are the only one who is asked to dance out of your group of friends. How do you feel? How do they feel? How do you accept or reject the invitation nicely?

   c. What happens in a situation when you are the only member of the opposite sex around? What are some appropriate ways to deal with this?

2. Peer feedback is important for those in the class who don't know how to act or what are the accepted norms for the group.

Time: One to two class periods

Notes to Teacher:

A. Explain the concept "stream of consciousness" to your students. Relate how they can use this skill in their presentations.

B. Ask students for ideas for other situations they'd like to act out.

C. Make sure the class is supportive and doesn't laugh at the shy student or the one who may not have had any experience in this area. This is the reason why groups rather than an individual should be assigned the role.

MY FRIEND IS SPECIAL BECAUSE...

My friend is special because, when hard times are in,
She's there with her happy grin.
When I'm in need of a favor,
Nor, should I ask, nor should I fear
No matter how far, no matter how near.
Does she understand that I am different?
Does she realize I'm not always efficient?
She does, she does, that's why she's special.

My friend is special because
She shares the good times, and always will.
The question then, "Will I?"
"Does she want to?"
Or does she want to say goodbye?
But deep beneath my rusted thought
I know this line I would've never thought
The times when the whole world walks out,
Neither do I call, nor do I shout.
It is that time to thank my friend.
She'll always come 'til the end,
She's given me courage; she is so special.
She is unique, not artificial,
She makes my life worth living for,
I hope I love her evermore.

By Missy Welch
San Diego, CA

I'M WITH YOU

Subject: Drama and Communications   **Grade Level:** Senior High

Content Objective: Students will use body language to express support and acceptance of another person.

Social Objective: This activity will help students identify how they feel toward others.

Materials: • role playing task cards provided by teacher

Directions:
1. Students will be provided with a role-playing task card which they will improvise in front of the class without using any words.
2. At least two students will do each of the cards.
3. As a large group, the pairs will have the effectiveness or ineffectiveness of their body language evaluated.
4. In a class discussion, the teacher needs to point out the four aspects of body language: distance, eye contact, posture, and non-verbal facial gestures. Focusing on supportive behaviors, a chart can be made to pinpoint specific body gestures that one would use to illustrate support and acceptance of another.

Example:

Eye Contact	Posture	Distance	Non-verbal Facial
Look at person while speaking	Touch them	Sit or stand closer to them	Smile; act interested in them

---

5. Situations to use:
   a) You are walking down a sidewalk. A person in a wheelchair is coming your way. How can you show you are supportive or accepting by using body language?
   b) You're at a party. A good friend brings an exchange student from another country that doesn't speak English. He introduces you and then walks away. How can you make this person feel accepted and supported without words?

I'M WITH YOU

    c) You are sitting at the lunchroom table with your friends. Some-
one you've been wanting to get to know comes in and sits down
at the opposite end of the table from you. You can't talk
because you're too far apart. How would you show that person
you are accepting and supportive without seeming overanxious?

  6. Discuss reactions afterwards.

Time: One to two class periods

**Notes to
Teacher:**   Students might read a book or articles on body language and/or mime.

MOM AND DAD

Once they were so far away.
They'll be gone tomorrow,
But they're here today.
My parents always did say
That everything would be okay.
But why did I always hide
When my mother cried?
Why did I want to die
When my father knew I lied?
Yet I know that I am welcome
To stay with them,
'Cause they've always stood by me
When I was in need.
I wonder —
What would I be
Without my family?

By Fran Botos
San Diego, CA

157

EVERYTHING YOU ALWAYS
WANTED TO KNOW
BUT WERE AFRAID TO ASK

Subject: Drama and Communications   **Grade Level:** Jr. & Sr. High

Content Objective: Students will be more aware of voice tones. They will perfect their communication skills for gathering information.

Social Objective: Students will be provided with a medium to relate to peers on a positive note in order to help understand and accept differences in people. They will learn how to ask for "personal" information without insulting the other person.

Materials: • tape recorders

Directions: 1. Teachers will discuss with students appropriate methods to utilize when asking people personal questions. Teachers should provide their students with some models.

2. Students will be paired. A tape recorder per pair should be provided if available. Otherwise, the equipment can be passed around and shared.

   The task is for each student to ask his partner one question that he always wanted to know about but was afraid to ask. Partner has the option of passing and not providing the answer. Students will play back how they sound concentrating on tone of voice and clarity of information. Questions they should ask themselves are: a) How did they come across on the recorder? b) How do others hear them?

3. Next the teacher provides each pair with an index card and a situation. A list of possible situations appears below. The pair discusses together the best way to approach the situation on the card. Then they can demonstrate or act out the situation into the tape recorders.

   a. A person in a wheelchair.

   b. A person who doesn't celebrate Christmas.

   c. A person who grew up in another state.

   d. A person who is blind.

   e. A person with missing limbs.

EVERYTHING YOU ALWAYS
WANTED TO KNOW
BUT WERE AFRAID TO ASK

    f. A person who speaks more than one language.

    g. A person who celebrates a different holiday than you do.

4. The situation is then played back to the class. The class will react together as to whether they would have answered the question the way the original student dyads did. Constructive peer evaluation and feedback is encouraged.

Time: One to two class periods or longer if deemed valuable

IT HURTS

It hurts when I say, "Hello" and I hear no reply.
It hurts when I stand there with a group passing by.

They think I don't notice but it stares me in the face.

It hurts when you laugh and I know not why.
It hurts when they avoid me; it makes me want to cry.

It hurts when I'm alone; they look at me and stare.
It makes me think they don't even care.

It hurts when they laugh when another jumps away from me.

It's not fair. But most of all, it hurts because
they're my friends and I'm not theirs.

By Tara Nicholson
Oceanside, CA

PAPER BAG DRAMATICS

Subject: Drama and Communications   **Grade Level:** Jr. & Sr. High

Content Objective: Students will participate in classroom dramas which demonstrate the knowledge of props and costuming.

Social Objective: This activity will facilitate the acceptance of others.

Materials: • materials listed below   • garbage bags (paper or plastic)

Directions: 1. Divide class into groups of 4-6 students.
2. Give each group a paper bag filled with props. On the paper bag put a label that relates to the theme of their skits.
3. Have groups explore the props in their bag.
4. Have group create and act out a five-minute skit using these props.
5. End the activity with a discussion of the stereotyping that may have surfaced in the skits.

Possible Props for Skit about Handicapped Individuals
a) Glasses that you can't see out of
b) A cane
c) A sling
d) Cap
e) Book
f) Pencil

Possible Props for Skits about Racial Stereotypes
a) Afro-pick
b) Hairnet
c) Transistor radio
d) White T-shirt
e) Hats
f) Pack of cigarettes
g) Ball

Posssible Props for Skits about Sexual Discrimination
a) Makeup
b) Dress
c) High heels
d) Vest
e) Male hat
f) Male belt
g) Toothpick

Possible Props for Skits about Age Discrimination
a) Wig
b) Spectacles
c) Powder
d) Shawl
e) Watch
f) Pill box
g) Deck of cards

Time: One to two class periods

Notes to Teacher: Time for discussion is important.

FRIENDSHIP DAY

Subject: Social Science   **Grade Level:** Junior High

Content Objective: Students will actively participate in a movement to make a change in today's society.

Social Objective: Students will identify important characteristics of a friendship as well as widen their opportunity for making new friends.

Materials:
- letter writing paper
- addresses of Congresspersons
- envelopes

Directions: Students will write a letter to their Congressperson suggesting the development of a National Friendship Day. In their letters, students should specify *why* they feel this is important. They should also include suggestions for ways to observe this holiday on

     a. an individual basis

     b. a national basis

     c. an international level

        or

As a class, they could proclaim a day of friendship and decide how they're going to implement it. How can they get the school involved?

Time: Two to three class periods or a unit of study

Notes to Teacher: A. As an offshoot of the observance of Friendship Day, students can start a pen-pal relationship with students in another country.

B. Have students contact the United Nations or the American Field Service Organization (foreign student exchange) for information on how to become an exchange student as well as how to apply for one to visit.

MY FRIEND IS SPECIAL

My friend is special because she helps me out in everything I do, especially when I'm down or sad. She cheers me up if I'm in a bad mood. She's funny, cool, and nice. She makes me laugh all the time. I like to hang around with her because she's friendly.

When she comes over to my house, she acts like a sister sometimes. She eats dinner with me and stays over for the night. My parents get along with her and so do my sisters.

She is also special because she's just herself. She doesn't act another way just to impress me, and she doesn't talk behind my back. She is considerate to me and to other people. She is special to me in many other ways, but I can't name the reasons because they're infinite.

By Azella Caballero
Chula Vista, CA

PR FOR A CULTURE

Subject: Social Science   **Grade Level:** Jr. & Sr. High

Content Objective: Students will understand and respect American ideals and the American cultural heritage. They will identify that these values result from the contributions of many peoples and many cultures.

Social Objective: Students are provided an opportunity to focus on commonalities with a representative from their own school or class that they can relate to. This will help them develop a positive attitude toward others and their culture.

Materials:
- a regular textbook
- a student to act as public relations person for his/her culture
- the PR student should bring in any objects that he/she uses every day in his/her home which may be different from American tradition

Directions:
1. Encourage students to act as "Public Relations" persons for their or their relatives' culture. First have them identify the commonalities between their customs and those of the American society. This procedure is suggested because commonalities are what brings individuals together.
2. Once students have shared the commonalities, have them share the differences between their culture and the American culture.
3. Information that they might share are:

   a. food   f. clothing
   b. pictures   g. artifacts
   c. mementos   h. maps
   d. stories   i. types of jobs
   e. genealogy   j. exports

4. Students can bring in objects that they feel are representative of their cultures to share with classmates.
5. After a student's presentation, a discussion should ensue. Desks should be arranged in a circle to facilitate the informal discussion and understanding.

Time: One class period to a week, depending on number of students who wish to share their heritage

TRADITION

Subject: Social Science   **Grade Level:** Jr. & Sr. High

Content Objective: Students will develop an understanding and appreciation of the culture of persons of diverse racial and ethnic backgrounds.

Social Objective: This activity will promote a positive change in students' attitudes, feelings, and actions toward others.

Materials: • paper   • pencil   • chalkboard

Directions: 1. Students will individually list ways that their family celebrates a particular holiday such as July 4th, New Year's Day, or birthdays. Students might tell about foods they eat, special activities, games they play, gifts and decorations, religious involvement. They will make a list of things they do or write a paragraph about the holiday including the information.

2. All students will compare their lists and focus on commonalities. These commonalities should be listed on the chalkboard.

3. Students having different answers should be given class time to discuss the origin of their particular tradition. They can share why their family celebrates in that way.

4. Questions to consider:

   a) How are your celebrations like other class members?

   b) What things would you change?

   c) What things would you keep the same?

Time: 1-3 class periods

Notes to Teacher: A. Have students research how different holidays are celebrated around the world.

B. This is a good activity to do around holiday season.

164

WEEK OF FAVORS

Subject: Social Science   **Grade Level:** Junior High

Content Objective: Students will develop a commitment to responsible citizenship by changing their own actions.

Social Objective: This activity is geared to expand the individual's positive interactions with others as well as to evaluate the results of one's actions.

Materials: • form

Directions:

1. The task for students is to choose a different individual from one of the five areas below to volunteer their services or to demonstrate a positive action such as saying something positive, sharing the responsibility of a chore or doing something the other person enjoys.

   a) an elderly person

   b) a younger person

   c) a family member

   d) a classmate

   e) an adult they see daily (parent, teacher, bus driver)

2. This would be a good homework assignment.

3. Have students record their actions on a form similar to the one below:

Favors I Have Done for Others			
Who	What You Did	What Happened	Why It Happened
Monday			
Tuesday			
Wednesday			
Thursday			
Friday			

4. At the end of the week discuss what they have done to help others. Relate their actions to ways in which they can be good and responsible citizens.

Time: 5-10 minutes of time daily for one week

MOCK ELECTION

Subject: Social Science   **Grade Level:** Junior High

Content Objective: Students will become aware of the aspects of the democratic process of election.

Social Objective: This activity fosters positive interpersonal relationships between classmates.

Materials: None

Directions: Students will draw a classmate's name out of a hat. Pairs will get together and try to find out as many positive reasons why the rest of the class should vote for their partner for "ACATEK." They will then act as campaign managers for each other doing the following activities:

   a. Students will interview each other to get information.

   b. Students will make a campaign poster about their partner.

   c. Students will do a five minute introduction or speech why this person should be elected head "ACATEK" in front of the class.

Time: One week

Notes to Teacher:

A. This is a good activity around election time. Use of a nonsense word for this campaign enables the students to learn the election process without interference of preconceived connotations. Often the standard offices held, i.e., President, Vice President, etc., carry with them feelings of previous failure or a popularity contest.

B. A supplementary activity might be to go to a local campaign headquarters and find out the types of activities actually done in campaigning.

C. If you wanted to put some real competition into it you can recognize the partners who do the best job publicizing, etc. Teamwork really helps.

D. If students really get involved in the process, they can put on their own convention.

I'VE HAD THE SAME JOB

Subject: Career Education   **Grade Level:** Jr. & Sr. High

Content Objective: Students will become familiar with job opportunities available for their age level.

Social Objective: Students will focus on similarities and work together in a spirit of positive communication.

Materials: None

Directions:
1. Divide class into groups of 4-6 students. Have them each share with group members jobs that they have had — paid and/or volunteer. Have them see if they can come up with at least one job the entire group has done.

2. The class will then get back together to develop a list of all the jobs students have done. Next, the class should discuss the jobs they liked and disliked and why.

3. End the class period by having students share their reactions to the following questions:
   a. What makes a job satisfactory?
   b. What are the benefits of volunteer work?
   c. What are the most desirable jobs for their age group and why?

Time: One to two class periods

Notes to Teacher: This is a good activity for students to get to know one another better. Similar feelings will surface.

WANTED: A FRIEND

Subject: Career Education   **Grade Level:** Junior High

Content Objective: Students will become familiar with want ads in the newspaper, how to read them, and what to look for. Students will begin looking at themselves and others realistically matching their own strengths with those that may appear in the want ads.

Social Objective: Students will explore their own attitudes, feelings, and actions toward others. This activity will provide models for students who do not know what's expected of them in order to be a good friend.

Directions:

1. Students will explore the Sunday paper want ads and choose 3-4 jobs they think they would qualify for or be interested in.

2. They are to cut out the ad and paste it on a half-sheet of paper.

3. Next to each ad, they list the qualities they think would be necessary to get that job.

4. Students should star those qualities that they think they possess. (This could be homework.) They should underline the qualities they could learn which would enable them to do the job.

5. Students can develop a class list of components that appear in an effective want ad, such as: attention-getting phrase, the position, hours, place of employment, possible skills needed, and contact information.

6. Using this format, they will individually develop their own want ad. The twist to this assignment is to advertise for a friend. They write their own ad on a 5 x 7 index card.

   Example: Buddy Needed: female friend from school to confide in, to laugh with, share interests with (dancing, tennis, and boys). Needs to be trustworthy, caring, friendly, and have good personality, good sense of humor and like sports. Please contact: Janet Doe, Homeroom 502, Johnson High.

7. Students will then exchange cards with at least three classmates. The classmate will take a blank sheet of paper and divide it into three sections. In each section they are to write down the qualifications needed in that ad and the contact person. They are then to star(*) the ones they think they qualify for.

WANTED: A FRIEND

8. Out of the three ads, they are to choose the one they feel the most qualified for. Teacher can provide class time for students to meet the employer.

9. A culminating activity might be for the whole class to develop a common list of qualifications for a friend.

Time: Two class periods

Notes to Teacher: A follow-up activity could have students interview each other to form new friendships!

BEING PART OF THE GROUP

It's always been something I've noticed.
Something I've seen. I've felt —
wanting to belong.
It seems a trivial facet of everyday
Oh, but everyone needs the feeling of significance.
Maybe, just knowing or at least
Receiving an impression I belong
Is a matter of reassurance of my mere existence.
The world is a vast world.
It laughs, cries, teaches, listens, loves, hates.
I need to be aware that the world
does these things . . .with me.

By Cristina Gruta
San Diego, CA

169

GETTING ALONG WITH OTHERS

Subject: Career Education   **Grade Level:** Jr. & Sr. High

Content Objective: Students will familiarize themselves with communication skills needed on the job.

Social Objective: By helping with new students who arrive at school, students will practice positive interpersonal relationships.

Materials:
- butcher paper
- list of procedures to follow (this will be developed by the class)

Directions:
1. Begin the activity with a large group discussion as to which communication skills are usually important in a job. Have class in small groups brainstorm specifics and write suggestions on butcher paper attached to the wall.

2. Have students relate these suggestions to their own school environment, specifically how to acquaint the new student to their school and classes.

3. Afterwards as a large group, develop a list of procedures to be used by all students when they are assigned to introduce a new student.

Time: Two to three class periods

Notes to Teacher: Talk to your principal or guidance counselor about assigning your students the responsibility of introducing all new students to the school. Allow a different classmate to do the job for each new student. Hopefully by the end of the year all students will have had an opportunity to do this job.

SAY WHAT YOU MEAN
(USING POSITIVE STATEMENTS)

Subject: Career Education   **Grade Level:** Junior High

Content Objective: Students will identify communication skills that are important on the job as well as surviving in society.

Social Objective: Students will increase awareness in their choice of words when communicating their feelings. They will be aware of others' feelings.

Materials:
- 150 3" x 5" cards
- 15 decks of cards with 10 cards in each deck.

Directions:
1. Pair students and give each a deck of cards with negative statements written on them:

   a. Shut up!   f. Don't look at me like that!

   b. Go away!   g. Don't copy my work!

   c. Don't be late!   h. Don't lie!

   d. Don't "bug" me!   i. Don't touch me!

   e. Don't call me names!   j. Don't leave your work area!

2. Divide the cards so that each student in the pair takes five of the ten cards.

3. Student A will start by reading one of the cards. Then in a password-like fashion, student B will try to restate the same concept or idea in a positive way.

4. Partners continue in the same manner alternating reading, till they use all ten cards.

5. After they have done this, debrief the activity. Talk about how it makes them feel to hear the word "don't."

Time: One class period

Notes to Teacher:

A. One option is to have the pair write their positives on the backside of the index card. The class can get together at the end and make a list of ways of expressing the positive.

B. Learning disabled students have a tendency to use a lot of negative comments in their conversation. This is a good way to model the positive.

C. Students might develop some class rules and state them in a positive manner.

STAY IN SCHOOL

Subject: Career Education   **Grade Level:** Jr. & Sr. High

Content Objective: Students will realize how important education is to their eventual career choice.

Social Objective: This activity promotes positive relationships between peers.

Materials:
- large decorative box to collect letters
- bulletin board located in lunchroom
- poster board
- art material

Directions:
1. Begin activity by having a large discussion with the class as to why education is important relative to their career choice. Then have students look at some jobs more specifically and decide what school subjects are required as a prerequisite. Also have them discuss changing careers later in life and why they need a broader education.

   The goal for the outcome of this discussion is to make them realize how important it is to continue in school.

2. Ask students to look at some of the negative feelings that they have all had about education. Next, look at statistics of how many dropouts there are. Plan how the class can reach out and help fellow students who are in the process of making this decision.

Time: Two class periods or unit of study

Notes to Teacher:
A. Students might be encouraged to start a schoolwide campaign to educate people as to the importance of finishing school. Posters which illustrate the pros to finishing one's education can be set up throughout the school.

B. Students might set up an anonymous letter box in which students can ask for help or ask specific questions before making the final decision on dropping out. This box should be located in an inconspicuous place where the identity of the depositor would remain confidential. Taking these questions, the class could do a general bulletin board that would answer some of the questions or develop a public fact sheet for distribution.

LAB PARTNERS FOR THE WEEK

Subject: Science   **Grade Level:** Jr. & Sr. High

Content Objective: Students will focus on what their goals are relative to science. They will cooperate with each other to achieve a common goal.

Social Objective: This activity promotes positive interaction between lab partners and the rest of the class.

Directions:
1. Determine at the beginning of the semester who will be lab partners. Have partners sign up for sharing information about themselves and compiling a section of the bulletin board entitled "Lab Partners for the Week." Sometime before their assigned week, partners should get together to find out the following information about each other:

   a. A general biographical sketch.

   b. Specify what their strengths are (these can be in school, out of school, relative to science or not).

   c. Specify what their goals are relative to science class participation.

   d. A positive statement about their partners and their relationship in science class.

   This information can be presented in creative ways of the partners' choice. Some ideas are to have pictures made of the partners in action in the laboratory (or any picture) with cute captions underneath their picture.

2. Allow five minutes at the beginning or end of class for the "honored partners" to share the information.

Time: Ongoing project/five minutes once per week

GIVING OF YOURSELF

Subject: Science   **Grade Level:** Jr. & Sr. High

**Content
Objective:** Students will identify the specific structures and processes of the cardiovascular system.

**Social
Objective:** Students will identify the rewards and drawbacks of helping others.

Materials: • options available: Red Cross Agency, local hospital, books, films, school nurse, medical specialist

Directions: 1. After presenting the regular content concentrating on blood, circulatory system, and cardiovascular structure, bring in the human factors. Ask students to do one of these assignments:

a) visit a hospital

b) participate in a blood drive

c) research abnormalities and diseases related to blood such as:
leukemia
hemophilia
anemia
sickle cell anemia
Tay Sachs disease

2. Then use these OR similar questions to debrief their activities:

a) During a blood drive, the opportunity exists to give of yourself to another person. How does this make you feel? Do you think you would feel differently giving to a relative or friend as opposed to a stranger?

b) What happens if you give blood and it doesn't work? What can go wrong? How do you deal with this?

c) Factual information about the mechanics of giving blood — what do they do? Machines that they may use?

d) Who gives?

3. This same format can be applied to other content such as Cardiovascular Pulmonary Resuscitation (CPR) and first aid/life saving techniques.

Time: One class period and a homework assignment

174

SCIENCE ICE BREAKER

Subject: Science   **Grade Level:** Junior High

Content Objective: Students will identify observation skills of scientific method.

Social Objective: This activity allows social interaction between students who otherwise might not work together.

Materials: • Have student bring a potato for class   • paper   • pencil

Directions:

1. Have students observe "their potato" for a five-minute time period.

2. Have them jot down specific characteristics that will help them identify their potato.

3. After the time period has ended (e.g., 5 minutes), have students bring potatoes to the table in front of the room. Then have them go back to their seats.

4. Mix up the potatoes.

5. Ask each row of students to come up and pick out their potatoes.

6. Continue having all rows come to the table until all the potatoes are claimed.

7. Debrief this activity by having students discuss general characteristics that were helpful in their identification. They will say things like: color, size, smoothness, bruises, number of "eyes" and peculiar traits. Talk about their observation skills and how important they are in relation to the study of science.

8. Now have students get into groups by using one of the characteristics of their potato. Example: Those whose potatoes are smooth should get together, those whose potatoes have more than five "eyes," etc.

9. Keep groups for your planned activity for the day. You might have them compete as groups for the completion of the assignment.

Time: 15-20 minutes

Notes to Teacher:

A. This is an excellent warm-up activity to show the investigative process.

B. You might use this classification system as a creative way to dismiss the class that day.

SURVIVING

Subject:	Science

Grade Level: Jr. & Sr. High

Content Objective: Students will become aware of the interrelationship between Earth Science processes and their own environment.

Social Objective: Students will discuss methods for dealing with the human aspect of a natural disaster.

Materials:
- textbook
- filmstrip on earthquakes or volcanoes if available

Directions:

1. When studying the subject of disastrous physiological changes in the earth, bring in the human aspect of coping and what to do in an emergency. Discuss with students the general procedures that they should know before a disaster occurs. Talk about what they can do to help themselves, family, and neighbors.

2. Divide the class up into groups of 4-6 students each. Each group will simulate a natural disaster such as fire, flood, volcano, earthquake, tornado, hurricane, etc. Given that there is a strong possibility that this could happen in their neighborhood, ask them to devise a plan that deals with the following concerns:

   a. *Prevention:* What can you do as an individual and as a member of the community to prepare for such a disaster? (Examples: telephone network or contact free education services)

   b. *Intervention:* What can you do during the disaster to avoid damage to self, family, neighbors, and property?

   c. *Aftermath:* What are ways that you and your community can cope with personal and physical losses?

3. After groups write down their ideas, they can share them with the class OR they can publish their ideas in booklet form using dittos to provide information to those around them. They might place a copy in the school library since the compiled information should be of interest to all students.

Time: One to two class periods

Notes to Teacher:

A. Students might make their own relief maps and use them to simulate the disasters.

B. Students may have experienced disasters, allow time for them to share their reactions.

MY MOUNTAINS

Standing in the background,
The mountains crown the moonlit city.
Life in the mountains
Seems busy as anthills.
Bees buzzing here,
or an eagle soaring there.
They will never go away.

The mountains are tall,
Like the buildings in my city.
They are bold and never ending.
Storms that blow over these mountains
Are like the shaking of salt over a potato.

People in my city
Never could stop appreciating
The security and the beauty
Of the mountains around my city.

Fran Botos
San Diego, CA

WANTED

Subject:	Science	**Grade Level:** Jr. & Sr. High

Content Objective: Students will develop skills in organizing data as a means for observation and physical identification.

Social Objective: The activity promotes the interaction between classmates in a positive manner.

Materials:
- 6 ink pads (1 per group) or water-soluble magic markers
- magnifying glass
- paper towels
- unlined white index cards
- 1 large envelope per group

Directions:

1. Divide the class into groups of six. Each person in the group will take an index card and put their thumbprint as neatly as possible in the middle of the card. Let it dry. Then put their card in the envelope. Students will then shake the envelope to mix up the cards.

2. The group will draw one card out at a time and place it on the table. Everyone puts their thumb on the table so that the group can inspect it with a magnifying glass. All thumbs should be touching with fingerprint facing upward.

3. The group will inspect the card with a magnifying glass to get familiar with identification lines, etc.

   The object is to come to a consensus concerning to whom that particular fingerprint belongs. As a person's thumbprint is identified, that hand is removed from the center. However, these students continue to be part of the guessing.

Time: One class period

Notes to Teacher: Another activity is for them to put their name on their card and design a character that looks like them doing a favorite science activity. These cards can be posted on the bulletin board or they can take them home. This is a fun activity.

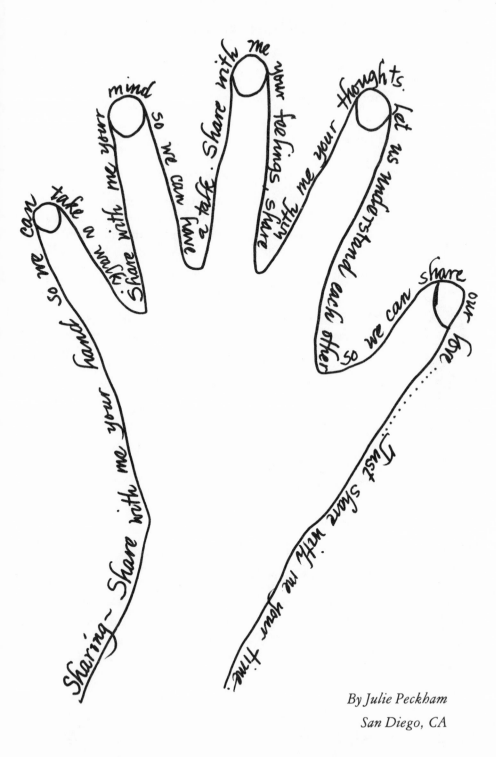

Sharing — Share with me your hand so we can take a walk. Share with me your mind so we can have a talk. Share with me your feelings, share with me your thoughts. Let us understand each other so we can share our love. Just share with me your time.

By Julie Peckham
San Diego, CA

HEROES IN OUR LIVES

Subject:	Physical Education **Grade Level:** Jr. & Sr. High
Content Objective:	Students will concentrate on sports heroes — winners and achievers in the field of sports. They will widen their concept of various sports including those in the lesser known categories.
Social Objective:	This activity helps students to recognize the strengths and similarities of different sports heroes. By concentrating on positive strengths and similarites in people, it is hoped that social barriers will begin to crumble.
Materials:	• bulletin board • sports magazines • newspapers • magazine articles • posters • collages
Directions:	Monthly bulletin board in the locker room will feature individuals from various minority populations. This will be an ongoing project throughout the year. Homework assignments could be delegated to a different class each month to contribute pictures and articles on the following topics:

1. Blacks Who Are Athletic Stars.
2. Handicapped People Who Are Winners.
3. Women in Sports.
4. Oriental and Asian Stars.
5. Mexican-American Champions.
6. Over 60 and Still Competing.
7. Teenagers in the Sports Spotlight.

Time:	Ongoing monthly project
Notes to Teacher:	A. A different topic can be the focus each month.
	B. A good activity geared toward heroes. This age group is known for identifying with heroes. Try to find ones who are good social models.

GIVING EVERYBODY A FAIR CHANCE

Subject: Physical Education   **Grade Level:** Jr. & Sr. High

Content Objective: Students will explain the concept of "handicapping" in sports.

Social Objective: This activity facilitates students in their inclusion and acceptance of individual differences relative to sports. Their strengths, weaknesses, and goals for improvements will be analyzed.

Materials:
- copies of golf card showing pars for holes
- diagram of placement for women-men tees

Directions:

1. Introduce the concept of "handicapping" by explaining how "handicaps" are defined in golf. Also bring in the idea of self improvement. Further clarify how two or more people of differing abilities can play the same game together and enjoy it.

2. After preparing the group toward an awareness of differing abilities and the rights of all individuals to play a sport, put the concept of "handicapping" into the game of the day.

3. Have students evaluate their performance relative to earning points for their team. They could average their scores over the past week. Have them handicap themselves on a scale of 1 to 5 according to their previous performance. "1" would stand for the highest performance and "5" for the lowest.

4. After students determine their "handicaps," teams would be chosen. Handicaps of all team members would be added to determine a "team handicap." Using the team handicap score, a decision should be made as to what score advantage one team would have to have over the other in order to win.

Time: One class period

Notes to Teacher: Another idea is to use this information to set up a tournament where similar ability students play each other. Winners from each group play another round.

SHAPING UP

Subject: Physical Education   **Grade Level:** Jr. & Sr. High

Content Objective: Students will experience a physical fitness program geared toward success. They will learn the basics of aerobic dance. Also, they will take their own and each other's pulse.

Social Objective: This activity will facilitate the acceptance and inclusion of all students and let each one shine.

Materials:
- record player or cassette
- record or cassettes of student's choice
- list of aerobic exercises

Directions:
1. Teacher should spend some time talking about aerobics and introducing basic activities and their purposes to the class.
2. Model exercises and teach students the basic movements of dances.
3. At the same time demonstrate how to take one's own and another's pulse.
4. After a week of teacher instruction and direction, the following procedure should be followed:
   a. Each student will pick two other classmates before class to take a resting pulse on.
   b. After the pulse-taking activity, two students who have been grouped by the teacher (with diverse abilities) will lead the aerobic routine for the day using music and steps that they have developed for homework.
   c. Following the dance routine, a record of pulse rates will be recorded when students reunite. Summarize and include in lesson with their partners of the day.
   d. This procedure will vary every day according to aerobic exercise leaders and pulse takers.

Time: Unit of study — aerobic dance

Notes to Teacher:
A. Everybody by the end of the semester will have taken and charted everyone else's pulse. It is hoped that this activity will encourage interaction and inclusion of all classmates.
B. Everyone will have a chance to lead the group and shine.
C. The importance of cooperation and common goals should surface.
D. Other benefits of this lesson are weight loss, sense of accomplishment, and improved coordination.
E. A radio can be used if a record or tape is not available.

WARMING UP TO ONE ANOTHER

Subject: Physical Education   **Grade Level:** Jr. & Sr. High

Content Objective: Students will physically warm up for the game of the day, week, or the unit.

Social Objective: Getting to know classmates — coming up with commonalities.

Materials
- large ball or frisbee, e.g. volleyball, football, tennis

Directions: This is a list of five minute activities that can be used to introduce a unit, get the year started, or help students warmup for daily activities.

1. At the beginning of the year have students throw a ball to a person they don't know. Ask them not to throw the ball to anyone who's caught it before. The goal is for everyone to catch the ball at least once.

2. The second time around students should throw the ball to the same person, say their name, and the person's name who threw it to them.

3. The third time around, ask students to throw the ball to a person whose name begins with the same letter as their name or the next letter alphabetically.

4. For line-ups or team formation, have students participate in order of:

   birthdays   shoe size   horoscope sign
   hand size   height   phone numbers

5. Do some general warm-up exercises that require two people working together. Examples:

   a. sit-ups — one person doing, the other person holds feet and counts.

   b. jumping jacks — face one another and try to do them in unison.

   c. activities that create physical resistance such as back-to-back, arms together.

6. Make sure that students team up with someone different every day.

Time: Ten to fifteen minutes

Notes to Teacher: Since the goal is to help students learn classmates' names, have them get in a circle two days a week at the beginning of class and do some warm-up exercises. Ask a different student to lead each activity.

RAINY DAY ROUNDUP

Subject: Physical Education   **Grade Level:** Jr. & Sr. High

**Content
Objective:** Students will learn to relate sports to their daily lives.

**Social
Objective:** This activity promotes the acceptance and inclusion of classmates.

Materials: Varies

Directions: The following activities can be used on rainy days when students cannot go outside:

1. *P.E. Jeopardy Game*

   Teacher would develop a jeopardy game using five different categories with five questions in each category. Questions should be taken from rules and procedures of games they've played during the semester. Teacher ranks questions on scale of 10, 20, 30, 40, and 50, according to their difficulty level. Teacher then divides class into two teams. The first person on the team takes the first question which is equal to 10 points and is from a category of his choice. If he gets it correct, he can answer another question or choose a teammate to answer for him. Teacher will keep track of points.

   Note: The student who doesn't have good coordination skills and may not shine on the field, may know the rules and can do well.

2. Bring in ink pads, paper, pens, colored pencils, and fine-pointed magic markers. Pair students up with classmates they do not know. Have them interview one another to find out sports their partner likes to participate in, watch, or both. Students then take fingerprints of their partner and make characters that represent their partner doing the sports. Limit to 5-6 characters. Display final products on bulletin board for all to see. Make sure names of partners are included on the final papers.

   *Note:*Teacher may wish to group similar interest students so commonalities are highlighted.

3. Show films or filmstrips like the ones from *Hello, Everybody* series. They show handicapped students succeeding in sports.

Time: One class period

FINDING NEW DOORS:

OTHER RESOURCES

CHAPTER VII

FINDING NEW DOORS: OTHER RESOURCES

Chapter VII

This chapter provides teachers with a list of commercially available materials and resources directly related to the three major goals of the book. For purposes of accessibility and organization, they are also classified according to the six subject areas used in the book. Included in the list are books, media, kits, and games of relevance to each goal and subject. The publisher's names are provided within the listing; however, their addresses can be found on pages 201-202.

In Section D of this chapter, an annotated bibliography of young adult fiction has been included for convenience sake. These are books teachers will be interested in referring to while implementing the lessons in *Unlocking Doors to Self-Esteem*.

Hopefully, this chapter will provide further direction toward maintenance of an accepting and positive classroom environment.

FINDING NEW DOORS: OTHER RESOURCES

A. Resources Fostering Positive Self-Concepts

ENGLISH

1. **The Search for Self in Literature**   multi-media kit
   Guidance Associates

   In this program students explore the literature of self discovery and
   examine concepts of individual identity. Works used include **Alice
   in Wonderland, Soul Catcher, Siddhartha,** and writings from
   Thoreau, Dickinson, Baldwin, Lessing, Whitman, Shakespeare, and
   Toni Mitchell.

2. **TA for Teens**   book or cassette
   Jalmar Press

   This book by Dr. Alvyn M. Freed is geared towards adolescents and
   their common dilemmas. Applied Transactional Analysis techniques are helpful with self concept and interpersonal relationships.

DRAMA AND COMMUNICATIONS

1. **Am I OK?**   posters
   Argus Publishers

   These colorful posters are geared toward secondary students. They
   can be adapted for creative writing, role playing, or bulletin boards.

2. **Do It Yourself Critical and Creative Thinking**   book
   Resources for the Gifted

   A book designed to build self esteem because it is written with the premise: "I know more than I thought." The outcome is an open ended scrapbook of ideas, thoughts, and observations about the student's creative and critical thinking skills.

3. **100 Ways to Enhance Self Concepts in the Classroom**   book
   Prentice-Hall, Inc. *(Distributed by B.L. Winch & Associates)*

   A handbook for teachers and parents by Jack Canfield and Harold C. Wells. It includes more than 100 excellent ideas for building positive self-concepts in all students.

4. **The Sharing Game**   board game
   B.L. Winch and Associates

   A semi-structured, non-threatening, enjoyable way to involve students in communicating with each other. The game fosters exploration of likenesses and differences and helps students gain a better awareness of themselves and others.

SOCIAL SCIENCE

1. **Developing Self-Respect**   multi-media kit
   Learning Tree

   Real life dramatizations show students that self respect develops out of self awareness and the willingness to take responsibility for one's own behavior. Could be infused into units on citizenship and government.

2. **How Do I See Myself?**   multi-media kit
   Sunburst Communications

   Dramatizations of real teenage experience to help students honestly examine their own self images and recognize the influences that affect these self perceptions. Practical guidelines are given for recognizing and changing undesirable personality traits.

SCIENCE

1. **The Problem — Acne**   multi-media kit
   Hubbard

   The problem of acne is discussed openly and honestly. Feelings of
   being self-conscious are dealt with. A follow-up activity could lead
   into self concept activities.

2. **Self Care Series — Female**   multi-media
   Self Care Series — Male
   Hubbard

   Practical guides to personal grooming for today's adolescents.
   Methods and techniques shown reflect a multi-ethnic emphasis.
   Contemporary language and music helps maintain interest.

3. **'Me Now' Science and Health Program**   curriculum guides
   Hubbard

   This program develops a basic understanding of the body and how it
   works. Activity-centered and multisensory approach is encouraged.
   Studying one's body is a natural jump-off point to greater self
   awareness and self esteem.

4. **Overcoming Handicaps**   multi-media kit
   Learning Tree

   This series will help mainstreamed students deal with the problems
   they face everyday and give them a more positive perspective of their
   own futures. Could be used for peer exposure and awareness.

5. **Being You**   multi-media kit
   Learning Tree

   Presents a difficult concept artistically and well.

6. **Take Care of Yourself**   book
   Quercus Corporation

   This book provides practical suggestions for basic body care involving
   diet, rest, and exercise.

189

CAREER EDUCATION

1. **Job Survival Skills**   multi-media
   Singer Publishing Co.

   An extensive program designed to help students develop personal and interpersonal skills most frequently needed to find and keep a good job. A large group of coordinated materials to give students a foundation for communication skills. It also helps them develop positive self concepts which facilitate interactions with their employers and fellow employees.

2. **If You Don't Know Where You're Going, You'll
   Probably End Up Somewhere Else**   book
   Argus Publishers

   A paperback that helps students in grades 7-12 explore their skills in goal setting that relate to career decision making.

3. **Develop the Whole Person to Build a Better Tomorrow**
   Argus Publishers

   Life Centered Educational Materials.

PHYSICAL EDUCATION

1. **Understanding Yourself**   multi-media kit
   Harvest Educational Labs

   This series is designed to establish a more balanced self-evaluation, to recognize the positive characteristics of each individual, and seek assistance in overcoming weaknesses.

2. **Teen Scenes**   posters
   Developmental Learning Materials (DLM)

   Handicapped teenagers are pictured in work and recreational settings. Very good for bulletin boards because it promotes feelings of competence, positive self concept, and encourages acceptance and respect for individual differences and similarities.

B. Resources Exploring Attitudes, Feelings and Actions Toward Others

ENGLISH

1. **The Ungame**   game
   The Ungame Company

   A noncompetitive game that encourages players to communicate their feelings and interests to each other in a nonthreatening manner.

2. **Getting It Together — A Reading Series About People**   readers
   Science Research Associates (SRA)

   The series features life problem themes. How to deal with personal problems and interpersonal relationships comprises the content of the lessons. Reading comprehension is stressed.

3. **Prejudice in Literature**   filmstrips
   Guidance Associates

   These filmstrips present causes and consequences of prejudice related to race, religion, age, sex, political beliefs, and class. How to resist prejudices is discussed.

4. **Courage in Literature**   filmstrips
   Guidance Associates

   Western ideas of courage in spiritual struggle, principled resistance, physical exploits, holocaust survival, nonconformity, openness to change, and the unknown are traced through literary works such as Donne, Hawthorne, Defoe, Ginsberg, Heyerdahl, Sillitoe, and Baldwin, among others.

5. **Lifeline**   kit
   Argus Communications

   Helps students understand the needs, feelings and opinions of others. Students are involved in value dilemmas requiring them to make decisions and to examine the consequences of their choices.

DRAMA AND COMMUNICATIONS

1. **Can of Squirms**   role-playing activities
   Arthur Meriwether, Inc.

   Designed for junior-senior high school students to role-play pro-
   vocative real-life situations. These experiences help them clarify and
   understand their own attitudes, values and needs, as well as to improve their communication skills.

2. **Imagine**   game
   Arden Press

   A noncompetitive game which helps participants become more
   creative while learning more about their own emotions and attitudes.

3. **Dilemma**   kit
   Creative Learning Systems

   Simulation activities which focus on the ethics of group decision
   making as well as the effects of different leadership styles and the
   ways that prejudice can distort the process.

4. **Focus on People**   booklets
   Educational Insights

   These materials are designed to help the reader understand
   American Black, Latin, and Indian cultures. Topics such as history,
   literature, famous people, music, and dance are discussed.

5. **Black Leaders of Twentieth Century America**   cassettes
   BFA Educational Media

   This set of cassettes tells stories about black men and women of the
   twentieth century who have become leaders while overcoming personal and social adversities.

6. **The Nature of Prejudice**   book
   Addison-Wesley

   This book defines the roots and nature of prejudice.

SOCIAL SCIENCE

1. **Social Consequences at School**   filmstrip/cassette
   Interpretive Education

   This program focuses on the need to think before acting. It explores how responsibility, authority, and peer group pressure can affect different social situations occurring in school.

2. **Value Clarification**   book
   Hart Publishing Company

   Teacher book which guides students in evaluating their value systems as well as becoming more aware of their feelings.

3. **Values**   duplicating masters
   Educational Insights

   Designed for grades 7-12 to help students clarify their values and skills for getting along with others.

4. **Man: A Cross-Cultural Approach**   multi-media program
   Educational Design, Inc.

   Comprehensive filmstrip/cassette program which focuses students on recognizing universal similarities of experiences and attitudes of different cultures. Students develop a better understanding of themselves as well as an acceptance of others.

5. **Points of View**   cards
   Argus Communications

   These cards depict situations in which there are conflicting viewpoints. Students learn to examine both sides and to resolve the conflicts in an appropriate manner. Conflicts presented are ones dealing with race, sex, age, culture, and politics.

6. **We, the American Women**   book
   A Documentary History

   This book focuses on the historical contributions of women in the building of our nation.

7. **Rights and Responsibilities** cassettes
   BFA Educational Media

   This set focuses on how our Bill of Rights evolved and evaluates its relevancy to contemporary issues.

8. **Living in the Future: Now — Social Directions** cassettes
   BFA Educational Media

   These cassettes help viewers realize they have control over their lives now and in the future.

9. **America: Land of Change** book
   Science Research Associates (SRA)

   These six paperback books discuss the growth of America and how all its people gained their rights and power.

10. **Our Story: Women of Today and Yesterday** paperback books
    Science Research Associates (SRA)

    This paperback series presents the contributions to society by women through the ages.

11. **The 'Me' in Media** book
    Wieser Educational

    This book guides students in evaluating mass media and its effect on their thinking.

12. **Martin Luther King: The Search for Black Identity** filmstrips /
    Guidance Associates, Inc. cassettes

    This program offers historical perspective on the modern civil rights movement and the philosophy of non-violent action. Dr. King's philosophy of war, poverty, and workers' rights are presented.

13. **Handicapism and Equal Opportunity: Teaching About** book
    The Disabled in Social Studies
    Foundation for Exceptional Children

    This guide provides insight into attitudes and policies regarding the handicapped. It also fosters consciousness of one's own attitudes as well as those of society toward the disabled.

14. **Sensitivity**   cards
    Argus Communications

    These humorous cards focus on contemporary problems that are
    prominent among teenagers.

SCIENCE

1. **Understanding Your Feelings**   filmstrip
   Learning Tree

   These filmstrips present open-ended situations for which students
   discuss ways to express their emotions in accepted ways.

2. **"Facts About" Packet**   booklets
   Science Research Associates (SRA)

   This series deals with contemporary social problems — such as alcohol, drugs, and venereal disease — that high school students face.
   Factual information is presented without moralizing on the issues.

CAREER EDUCATION

1. **Living Skills**   cards
   Milton Bradley

   This six-unit interdisciplinary program uses value clarification
   techniques to encourage students to express their ideas. Topics such
   as awareness of basic social and economic decisions, self-direction,
   and realistic demands made by society are presented.

2. **Junior Guidance Series Booklets**   booklets
   Science Research Associates (SRA)

   This series covers topics that provide educational, vocational, personal, and social guidance to junior high students.

PHYSICAL EDUCATION

1. **Consequences**   cards
   Development Learning Materials (DLM)

   These cards present common social problems with which junior high
   and high school students are confronted daily.

C. Resources Facilitating Positive Social Interactions

ENGLISH

1. **Communicating Day by Day**   multi-media
   Harvest Educational Labs

   The why and how of effective interpersonal communications is demonstrated in home, school, social, and work situations. This program explains how people understand each other by speaking and hearing, reading, and writing clearly.

2. **Communicating to Make Friends**   book
   B.L. Winch and Associates

   This step by step program developed by C. Lynn Fox, Ph.D., is designed to aid elementary personnel in implementing peer acceptance and involvement in regular classrooms. A major influence in the development of this book.

3. **Feeling Free**   book
   Addison-Wesley

   A book of short stories, hard facts, photographs, and activities to help introduce kids (and adults) to their disabled peers. A frank, realistic approach to dealing with differences.

4. **Going Places with Your Personality**   workbooks
   Fearon-Pitman Learning, Inc.

   These are high-interest, low vocabulary worktexts designed to help students develop positive interpersonal habits. "What if this happened to you?" is used as the major approach.

5. **Effective Communication**   cassette
   Argus Publishers

   This program teaches 7-12th graders how to listen effectively as well as ways to evaluate their speech mannerisms.

DRAMA AND COMMUNICATIONS

1. **Person-to-Person**   book set
   Creative Learning Systems, Inc.

   This unique easelbook system structures communication between
   two students and helps them develop meaningful interaction skills.
   Students learn how to listen and really hear what another person is
   trying to say.

2. **Mainstreaming: What Every Child Needs
   to Know About Disabilities**   book
   The Exceptional Parent Press

   Excellent ideas to foster a relationship between the non-handi-
   capped and handicapped students.

3. **What's the Difference: Teaching Positive Attitudes
   Toward People with Disabilities**   book
   Human Policy Press

   It is a book filled with ideas to support acceptance of the handicapped.

4. **Roll-A-Role**   game
   The Ungame Company

   This game motivates students to apply effective communication
   skills to specific real life situations. Pairs of players roll character
   cubes to determine their roles, use chart to set location, and draw a
   topic card to establish the situation.

5. **The Big Hassle (and other Plays)
   The Put Down Pros (and other Plays)**   books
   Janus Publishing Company

   These books are filled with short, humorous plays depicting situations with which students can identify. They focus on interpersonal
   relationships and getting along with authority and with peers.
   Following each play are vocabulary building and writing activities.

6. **Me and Others**   multi-media
   Educational Designs, Inc.

Emphasis throughout this extensive program is on the acquisition of skills which help students become sensitive to the emotions of others and aware of those same emotions in themselves. The kit includes cassettes, filmstrip, activity books, role playing, and simulation activities.

7. **Developing Better Personal Relationships**   program
   Argus Publishers

This is a program for 11th and 12th graders to facilitate their understanding and skills in communicating with parents, friends, and teachers. Students develop personal journals as part of the program.

SOCIAL SCIENCE

1. **Social Consequences Series**   multi-media
   Interpretive Education

Hypothetical problem situations are drawn from home, school, and work settings. This program is designed to help students make intelligent decisions and evaluate their consequences.

2. **Social Consequences — Overview**   multi-media
   Interpretive Education

A broad overview of social consequences series is presented. Pertinent examples set the stage for topics covered in subsequent programs.

3. **Using Values Clarification**   film
   Media Five Films

Dr. Sidney Simon presents this documentary discussing the development and meaning of Values Clarification and demonstrating strategies involved with a group of high school students. He also describes how teachers can make valuing strategies a regular part of their school day.

4. **Including Me**   film
   Media Five Films

Through the stories of six young people, this film expresses the desire and legal right of handicapped persons to all the rich and fulfilling details of life. The common theme throughout the film is the fact that handicapped children are more like than unlike their peers, and that given equal educational opportunity, they have every chance to be as self-fulfilling as anyone else.

5. **Understanding Differences** multi-media
   Learning Tree

Throughout this presentation, a balance tone is maintained to help normal and handicapped children better understand and appreciate each other. Aids in exposure and fostering of important discussions.

SCIENCE

1. **Accepting Individual Differences** story flip books
   Developmental Learning Materials (DLM) guides and cassette

The overall premise of this program is that handicaps are simply extensions of individual characteristics found in all people. Student activities consist of sequential discussions and game-like activities centered around four themes: people are alike in some ways but also differ; people learn in different ways; even though we are different, we like each other; and people's appearances seem significant only when we don't know them.

2. **Hello Everybody** filmstrips and book
   James Stanfield Film Associates

Introduces handicapped children to peers and adults. Helps people to understand what life is like to people that have certain handicaps. Six different sound filmstrips, each concentrating on a person with a different handicap.

3. **People You'd Like to Know** film
   Encylopedia Britannica

It is an enjoyable film about understanding and accepting individuals with various handicapping situations.

CAREER EDUCATION

1. **On-The-Job Skills**   filmstrips
   Hampden

   Title of Filmstrip: Getting Along at Work.
   Students are introduced to social skills necessary for good interpersonal interaction on the job. Worker characteristics expected by employers and co-workers are emphasized.

2. **You and Others on the Job**   reading series (books)
   New Readers Press

   These relevant paperbacks show how different people cope with their work-related problems. The realistic stories open the way for students to explore their fears of inadequacy or feelings of overconfidence. Interpersonal skills are learned while reading comprehension is enhanced.

3. **Interpersonal Life Skills**   multi-media
   Singer Educational Division

   This extensive program provides true-to-life activities to help students learn to: a. Develop and maintain a positive self image, b. Evaluate how their words and actions affect others, c. Improve verbal and non-verbal expressive and receptive communication, and d. Modify their communication style to respond to needs of others.

PHYSICAL EDUCATION

1. **Play Fair: Everybody's Guide to Noncompetitive Play**   book
   Impact Publishers

   This book is an innovative resource for teachers who want to build cooperation as opposed to competition in their physical education classes.

2. **The New Games Book**   book
   The Headlands Press, Inc.

   This book provides descriptions of games in which everyone wins. These games effectively minimize sex and special skill considerations. They encourage basic feelings in non-threatening ways.

D. Publishers' Addresses

Addison - Wesley Publishing
Reading, MA 01867

Arden Press
P.O. Box 2084
Palm Springs, CA 92262

Argus Communications
7440 Natchez
Niles, Illinois 60648

Arthur Meriwether, Inc.
P.O. Box 457
Downers Grove, Illinois 60515

BFA Ed Media
2211 Michigan Avenue
P.O. Box 1795
Santa Monica, CA 90406

B.L. Winch and Associates
45 Hitching Post Drive, Bldg. 2
Rolling Hills Estates, CA 90274

Creative Learning Systems, Inc.
936 "C" Street
San Diego, CA 92101

Developmental Learning
Materials (DLM)
7440 Natchez
Niles, Illinois 60648

Educational Design, Inc.
47 West 13th Street
New York, N.Y. 10011

Educational Insights
150 West Carob
Compton, CA 90220

Encylopedia Britannica, Inc.
425 North Michigan Avenue
Chicago, Illinois 60611

Exceptional Parent Press
Statler Office Building, Room 700
Boston, MA 02116

Fearon-Pitman Learning, Inc.
6 Davis Drive
Belmont, CA 94002

Foundation for Exceptional Children
1920 Association Drive, Suite 301
Reston, Virginia 22091

Guidance Associates Inc.
Communications Park, Box 3000
Mount Kisco, New York 10549

Hampden
Box 4873
Baltimore, MD 21211

Hart
719 Broadway
New York, New York 10003

Harvest Educational Labs
Newport, Rhode Island 02840

Hubbard Publishing Co.
P.O. Box 104
Northbrook, Illinois 60062

Human Policy Press
P.O. Box 127
University Station
Syracuse, New York 13210

Impact Publishers
P.O. Box 1094
San Luis Obispo, CA 93406

Interpretive Education
157 South Kalamazoo Mall
Kalamazoo, Michigan 49003

Jalmar Press
45 Hitching Post Drive, Bldg. #2
Rolling Hills Estates, CA 90274

James Stanfield Film Associates
P.O. Box 1983
Santa Monica, CA 90406

Janus Book Publishers
Hayward, CA 94545

Learning Tree
7108 S. Alton Way
Englewood, CO 80122

Milton Bradley
443 Shaker Road
East Long Meadow, MA 01028

New Readers Press
Box 131
Syracuse, New York 13210

Prentice Hall, Inc.
Box 500
Englewood Cliffs, New Jersey 07632

Quercus Corporation
2768 Pineridge Road
Castro Valley, CA 94546

Resources for the Gifted
3421 North 44th Street
Phoenix, Arizona 85018

SRA Science Research Associates
155 North Wacker Drive
Chicago, Illinois 60606

Singer Education Division
Career Systems
80 Commerce
Rochester, New York 14604

Sunburst Publications
Dept. TG
Pleasantville, New York 10570

The Ungame Company
1440 South State College Blvd.,
Bldg. 2-D
Anaheim, CA 92806

Wiser Educational
P.O. Box 538
El Toro, CA 92630

E. Annotated Bibliography of Young Adult Fiction
A Resource List for Teachers

Albert, Louise
But I'm Ready to Go, Bradbury Press, 1976, 230 pp.
> A slightly retarded 15-year-old girl tries to become a singer.

Allan, Mabel
The View Beyond My Father, Dodd, 1977, 192 pp.
> A 15-year-old discovers it is her father, as well as her blindness, that binds her to a narrow world.

Bawden, Nina
The Witch's Daughter, Lippincott, 1966, 181 pp.
> As they become involved in uncovering a gang of jewel thieves, a blind girl and her mother help a lonely orphan realize that her ability to see into the future is a special talent, not witchcraft.

Beckwith, Lillian
The Spuddy, Delacorte Press, 1976, 118 pp.
> In Scotland a lonely mute boy and a stray dog make friends with a kind sea captain.

Bradbury, Bianca
Lots of Love, Lucinda, Washburn, 1966, 171 pp.
> A good story of civil rights problems in the North.

Bradbury, Bianca
Nancy and Her Johnny-O, Washburn, 1970, 150 pp.
> An adolescent girl faces many problems having a 5-year-old retarded brother living at home.

Brown, Fern
You're Somebody Special on a Horse, A. Whitman, 1977, 128 pp.
> Marni may lose her beloved horse because her grades in school are low, but by helping in a program for handicapped riders she gains new insight into her own problems.

Brown, Roy
Escape the River, Seabury, 1970, 160 pp.
> Paul, an adopted child, and Kenny, his retarded brother, help with the family towing business on the Thames River.

Butler, Beverly
Gift of Gold, Dodd, 1972, 278 pp.
> A blind young woman confronts the possibility of having her vision restored.

Butler, Beverly
Light a Single Candle, Dodd, 1962, 242 pp.
The story of a girl's adjustment to blindness, which means learning to live with the attitudes of others as well as to control a seeing-eye dog.

Byars, Betsy
The Summer of the Swans, Viking, 1970, 142 pp.
Sara's 14th summer is filled with the uncertainty of growing up, until the night her retarded younger brother disappears.

Cavanna, Betty
Joyride, Morrow, 1974, 222 pp.
Susan battles polio during her four years of high school and tries to accept her handicap and her prospects for the future.

Chipperfield, Joseph
A Dog to Trust: The Saga of a Seeing-eye Dog, McKay, 1963, 181 pp.
A dog, Arno, is trained to become a seeing-eye dog for John Ash. Later Ash recovers his sight and must lead Arno who becomes blind.

Christopher, Matthew
Stranded, Little, Brown, 1974, 116 pp.
Shipwrecked with his dog on an uninhabited Caribbean Island after a hurricane that washed his parents overboard, a blind boy struggles for survival.

Cleaver, Vera
Me Too, Lippincott, 1973, 158 pp.
A 12-year-old tries to teach her retarded twin.

Cookson, Catherine
Go Tell It To Mrs. Golightly, Lothrop, 1977, 192 pp.
A blind girl who is staying with her grandfather stumbles upon a kidnapping in their small town.

Corcoran, Barbara
A Dance to Still Music, Atheneum, 1974, 180 pp.
Fourteen-year-old Margaret refuses to accept her brother's deafness and runs away in fear that her mother's remarriage may mean she'll be sent to a boarding school.

Field, Rachel
And Now Tomorrow, MacMillan, 1942, 350 pp.
Emily Blair becomes deaf on the eve of her marriage. The changes that ensue and the insight she gains through personal tragedy form a story of love and understanding.

Friis-Baastad, Babbis
Don't Take Teddy, Scribner, 1967, 218 pp.
>   Mikkel's older brother Teddy isn't like other boys. When Teddy accidentally knocks out a boy's teeth, Mikkel decides to run away with him to the mountains.

Garfield, James B.
Follow My Leader, Viking Press, 1957, 191 pp.
>   After being accidentally blinded by a firecracker, Jimmy learns to live a normal life with the help of Leader, his seeing eye dog.

Green, Hannah
I Never Promised You a Rose Garden, Holt, 1964, 300 pp.
>   This is the story of a schizophrenic teen-age girl and her struggle to deal with reality while being treated at a mental hospital.

Greenberg, Joanne
In This Sign, Holt, 1970, 275 pp.
>   Abel and Janice Ryder are both deaf. This book describes their struggles in the world of the hearing and the painful work of raising a hearing daughter.

Grohskopf, Bernice
Shadow in the Sun, Atheneum, 1975, 182 pp.
>   While visiting her aunt at Cape Cod, Fran accepts a job as a companion to a crippled girl whose unhappiness and frustration make their relationship a difficult one.

Haar, Jaapter
The World of Ben Lighthart, Delacorte Press, 1977, 123 pp.
>   Blinded by accident, a young boy decides to take control of his handicap and not permit it to keep him from his friends and family.

Heide, Florence
Growing Anyway Up, Lippincott, 1976, 128 pp.
>   With the help of her aunt, Florence is able to face a problem she has not recognized for years and adjust to changes in her life.

Hoff, Sid
Irving and Me, Harper, 1967, 226 pp.
>   Artie Granick, 13, is very unhappy over his family's moving and doesn't want to leave his friends. Then he finds Irving, also from the North, and life improves.

Keyes, Daniel
Flowers for Algernon, Bantam, 1966, 216 pp.
>   After being retarded for 32 years, Charlie Gordon undergoes an operation designed to change his life.

Koob, Theodora
The Deep Search, Lippincott, 1969, 188 pp.
Ten-year-old Paul Fontaine's family learns to live with and accept him as a mentally handicapped person.

L'Engle
The Young Unicorns, Farrar, 1968, 245 pp.
A little blind girl, her teenage reader, and their friends are under the cloud of some evil influence.

Little, Jean
Listen for the Singing, Dutton, 1977, 215 pp.
As WWII approaches, German-born Anna lacks confidence in herself, because of her very poor sight. Entering the regular Canadian high school, she discovers that she possesses special abilities and strengths.

Little, Jean
Mine for Keeps, Little, 1962, 186 pp.
Sally, crippled by cerebral palsy, walks with crutches. One day after years in a school for handicapped children, she comes home to an understanding family, a new puppy to train, and new friends.

Little, Jean
Take Wing, Little, 1968, 192 pp.
Burdened by her awareness that 7-year-old James is mentally retarded, Laurel is prodded by a bossy aunt and a stuck-up cousin into seeking friends and a normal life for herself.

MacIntyre, Elisabeth
The Purple Mouse, T. Nelson, 1975, 108 pp.
A girl with a hearing problem realizes that her struggle to overcome her handicap has made her a stronger and happier person.

Madison, Winifred
The Mysterious Caitlin McIver, Follett, 1975, 240 pp.
A conservative 16-year-old meets an unconventional Scottish girl and is drawn to her carefree, casual life styles.

Mathis, Sharon Bell
Listen for the Fig Tree, Viking, 1974, 175 pp.
A 16-year-old blind girl finds new strength when she explores her African heritage as she struggles to help her whiskey-drinking mother.

Maugham, W.
Of Human Bondage, Doubleday, 1936, 565 pp.
This book tells of thirty years in the life of Philip Carey as he searches for adjustment to a physical deformity. He suffers many temporary setbacks in his pursuit of a medical course.

Micklish, Rita
Sugar Bee, Delacorte Press, 1972, 195 pp.
  Sugar Bee leaves Pittsburgh for a week in the country with the Martins
  and their daughter Rosemary. Sugar Bee felt different because she was
  black, but soon discovered Rosemary was different, too, and love and
  friendship can wipe away barriers.

Neufeld, John
Lisa, Bright and Dark, Phillips, S.G., 1969, 125 pp.
  Sixteen-year-old Lisa Shilling is losing her mind and her only hope of
  help comes from her friends.

Platt, Kin
Hey, Dummy, Dell, 1971, 171 pp.
  Neil befriends the brain-damaged boy who just arrived in the
  neighborhood.

Quimby, Myrtle
The Cougar, Criterion Books, 1968, 128 pp.
  A young boy with an Indian mother and a white father must learn to fit
  into a world that is not ready to accept him.

Rodowsky, Colby
P.S. Write Soon, Watts, 1978, 149 pp.
  A physically handicapped girl uses her letters to a pen pal as an outlet for
  daydreams about her own life.

Savitz, Harriet May
The Lionhearted, John Day, 1975, 149 pp.
  Resigned to life in a wheelchair, Rennie reaches out to new friendships
  with an overweight girl and a handsome, popular senior boy.

Savitz, Harriet May
Run, Don't Walk, Watts, 1979, 122 pp.
  When a teenager returns to school in a wheelchair after an accident, all
  she wants is to be left alone. A handicapped activist insists, however, she
  join his crusade.

Sorenson, Virginia
Around the Corner, Harcourt, 1971, 186 pp.
  A black boy's mother forbids him to associate with the neighbors whom
  she considers "poor white squatters." Then she unexpectedly begins
  labor, and a number of misunderstandings are righted.

Stolz, Mary
By the Highway Home, Harper, 1971, 194 pp.
  Misfortune hits the Reed family, and everybody changes. First they learn
  of Cathy's brother Bean's death in Vietnam and then Cathy's father loses

his job. They are forced to accept charity and live with Cathy's Uncle Henry.

Storr, Catherine
Thursday, Harper, 1972, 274 pp.
A 15-year-old girl tries to help an emotionally-confused boy accept life's realities.

Taylor, Theodore
The Cay, Doubleday, 1969, 137 pp.
When the Germans torpedo the freighter on which Phillip and his mother are sailing from Curocao to the United States, only Phillip and an old West Indian survive. In their struggle, the boy depends on the wise old black man and learns to adjust to the blindness that has afflicted him.

Vinson, Kathryn
Run with the Ring, Harcourt, 1965, 255 pp.
After falling at a track meet where his only competitor is his bitter enemy, Mark Mansfield is blinded. Mark is convinced that Curt fouled him, and carries his bitterness with him into his new life at a special school. Rebuilding his ham radio station, learning Braille, and learning to sprint again now keeps Mark busy.

Whitney, Phyllis
Nobody Likes Trina, Westminster, 1972, 187 pp.
When Sandy moves from NYC to the country, she learns from the unpopular and shy Trina the value of friendship and a respect for nature.

Whitney, Phyllis
Secret of the Emerald Star, Westminster Press, 1964, 233 pp.
With Mrs. Devery resenting many strangers in the neighborhood and Stella feeling sorry for herself because of her blindness, Robin has quite a frustrating time, trying to be friendly with such unhappy neighbors.

Wilson, Holly
Double Heritage, Westminster Press, 1971, 172 pp.
In Detroit, in 1832, Emily, half Chippewa Indian, faces many hardships and prejudices while growing up.

Witheridge, Elizabeth
Dead End Bluff, Atheneum, 1966, 186 pp.
Story of a blind boy who is determined to do all the things other kids do.

Witter, Evelyn
Claw Foot, Lerner, 1976, 66 pp.
By learning to use his talents instead of dwelling on his handicap, Claw Foot, a lame Sioux Indian boy, earns a new name for himself.

F. References

Allport, G.W. *Personality and Social Encounter.* Boston: Beacon Press, 1960.

Bandura, A. & Walters. *Social Learning and Personality Development.* New York: Holt, Rinehart & Winston, 1963.

Bandura, A. & Walters. *Social Learning and Personality Development.* New York: Holt, Rinehart & Winston, 1963.

Berscheid, E. and Walster, E.H. *Interpersonal Attraction.* Reading, Massachusetts: Addison-Wesley, 1969.

Byrne, D. The Influence of propinquity and opportunities for interaction on classroom relationships. *Human Relations.* 1961, *14* 63-69.

Byrne, D. & Griffitt, W. Interpersonal attraction and similarity of personality characteristics. *Journal of Personality and Social Psychology.* 1973, *5,* 82-90.

Byrne, D., Griffitt, W. & Stefaniak, D. Attraction of personality characteristics. *Journal of Personality and Social Psychology.* 1967, *5,* 82-90.

Canter, L. & Carter, M. *Assertive Discipline.* Los Angeles: Canter & Associates, 1976.

Darley, J.M. & Berscheid, E. Increased liking as a result of the anticipation of personal contact. *Human Relations.* 1967, *20,* 29-40.

Elkind, D. *Children and Adolescents: Interpretive Essays on Jean Piaget.* New York: Oxford University Press, 1974.

Erikson, E. *Childhood in Society.* New York: Norton Publishing Co., 1950.

Fox, C.L. *Communicating to Make Friends: A Program for the Classroom Teacher.* Rolling Hills Estates, California: B.L. Winch & Associates, 1980.

Fox, C.L. & Malian, I.M. *Social Acceptance: Key to Mainstreaming.* Rolling Hills Estates, California: B.L. Winch & Associates, 1983.

Freed, Alvyn M. *TA for Teens.* Rolling Hills Estates, California: Jalmar Press, 1976.

Ginott, H. *Between Teacher and Child.* The Macmillan Company, 1972.

Gordon, T. *Parent Effectiveness Training.* New York: The New American Library, 1975.

Gordon, T. & Burch N. *Teacher Effectiveness Training.* New York: Peter H. Wyder, 1974.

Kehayan, V. Alex. *SAGE: Self Awareness Growth Experiences.* Rolling Hills Estates, California: Jalmar Press, 1990.

Muess, R.E. *Theories of Adolescence.* New York: Random House, 1965.

O'Connor, R.D. Relative efficacy of modeling, shaping, and the combined procedures for modification of social withdrawal. *Journal of Abnormal Psychology,* 1972, 79, 327-334.

Peretti, P. Social psychological aspects of students' acceptance and rejection. *Illinois School Journal.* 1973. 53, 30-35.

Zeigler, S. Demographic influences on adolescents' cross-ethnic friendship patterns: A four neighborhood study. Paper presented at annual convention of American Psychological Association, Sept. 1979. (ERIC Document reproduction service No. 179 890).

Openmind/Wholemind
Parenting & Teaching Tomorrow's Children Today

A book of powerful possibilities that honors the capacities, capabilities, and potentials of adult and child alike. Uses Modalities, Intelligences, Styles and Creativity to explore how the brain-mind system acquires, processes and expresses experience. Foreword by M. McClaren & C. Charles.
0-915190-45-1 $14.95
7 × 9   paperback
81 B/W photos   29 illus.

Present Yourself! *Captivate Your Audience With Great Presentation Skills*

Become a presenter who is a dynamic part of the message. Learn about Transforming Fear, Knowing Your Audience, Setting The Stage, Making Them Remember and much more. Essential reading for anyone interested in the art of communication. Destined to become the standard work in its field.
0-915190-51-6   paper $9.95
0-915190-50-8   cloth $18.95
6 × 9   paper/cloth. illus.

Unicorns Are Real
A Right-Brained Approach to Learning

Over 100,000 sold. The long-awaited "right hemispheric" teaching strategies developed by popular educational specialist Barbara Vitale are now available. Hemispheric dominance screening instrument included.
0-915190-35-4 $10.95
8½ × 11   paperback, illus.

Unicorns Are Real Poster

Beautifully-illustrated. Guaranteed to capture the fancy of young and old alike. Perfect gift for unicorn lovers, right-brained thinkers and all those who know how to dream. For classroom, office or home display.

JP9027 $4.95
19 × 27   full color

Imagination is the unicorn that lifts us above the mundane chains that bind the minds of many and flies us on fantastic wings to a place where dreams DO come true.

Practical Application, Right Hemisphere Learning Methods

Audio from Barbara Vitale. Discover many practical ways to successfully teach right-brained students using whole-to-part learning, visualization activities, color stimuli, motor skill techniques and more.
JP9110 $12.95
Audio Cassette

Don't Push Me, I'm Learning as Fast as I Can

Barbara Vitale presents some remarkable insights on the physical growth stages of children and how these stages affect a child's ability, not only to learn, but to function in the classroom.
JP9112 $12.95
Audio Cassette

Tapping Our Untapped Potential

This Barbara Vitale tape gives new insights on how you process information. Will help you develop strategies for improving memory, fighting stress and organizing your personal and professional activities.

JP9111 $12.95
Audio Cassette

Free Flight *Celebrating Your Right Brain*

Journey with Barbara Vitale, from her uncertain childhood perceptions of being "different" to the acceptance and adult celebration of that difference. A book for right-brained people in a left-brained world. Foreword by Bob Samples.
0-915190-44-3 $8.95
5½ × 8½   paperback, illus.

"He Hit Me Back First"
Self-Esteem through Self-Discipline

Simple techniques for guiding children toward self-correcting behavior as they become aware of choice and their own inner authority.
0-915190-36-2 $12.95
8½ × 11   paperback, illus.

Learning To Live, Learning To Love

An inspirational message about the importance of love in everything we do. Beautifully told through words and pictures. Ageless and timeless.
0-915190-38-9 $7.95
6 × 9   paperback, illus.

Pajamas Don't Matter:
(or What Your Baby Really Needs)

Here's help for new parents every-where! Provides valuable information and needed reassurances to new parents as they struggle through the frantic, but rewarding, first years of their child's life.
0-915190-21-4 $5.95
8½ × 11   paperback, full color

From Two To Three Years:
Social Competence

Shows important ways children define their identity by learning to play with other children, exploring the world, mastering the art of communication, and developing their senses of imagination and humor.
0-935266-03-8 $5.95
8½ × 11   paper, B/W photos

Feelings Alphabet

Brand-new kind of alphabet book full of photos and word graphics that will delight readers of all ages.''. . . lively, candid. . .the 26 words of this pleasant book express experiences common to all children.''
Library Journal
0-935266-15-1 $7.95
6 × 9   paperback, B/W photos

The Parent Book

A functional and sensitive guide for parents who want to enjoy every min-ute of their child's growing years. Shows how to live with children in ways that encourage healthy emo-tional development. Ages 3-14.
0-915190-15-X $9.95
8½ × 11   paperback, illus.

Aliens In My Nest
SQUIB Meets The Teen Creature

Squib comes home from summer camp to find that his older brother, Andrew, has turned into a snarly, surly, defiant, and non-communica-tive adolescent. *Aliens* explores the effect of Andrew's new behavior on Squib and the entire family unit.
0-915190-49-4 $7.95
8½ × 11   paperback, illus.

Hugs & Shrugs
The Continuing Saga of SQUIB

Squib feels incomplete. He has lost a piece of himself. He searches every where only to discover that his miss-ing piece has fallen in and not out. He becomes complete again once he discovers his own inner-peace.

0-915190-47-8 $7.95
8½ × 11   paperback, illus.

Moths & Mothers/
Feather & Fathers
A Story About a Tiny Owl Named SQUIB

Squib is a tiny owl who cannot fly. Neither can he understand his feel-ings. He must face the frustration, grief, fear, guilt and loneliness that we all must face at different times in our lives. Struggling with these feel-ings, he searches, at least, for understanding.

0-915190-57-5 $7.95
8½ × 11   paperback, illus.

Hoots & Toots & Hairy Brutes
The Continuing Adventures of SQUIB

Squib—who can only toot—sets out to learn how to give a mighty hoot. His attempts result in abject failure. Every reader who has struggled with life's limitations will recognize their own struggles and triumphs in the microcosm of Squib's forest world. A parable for all ages from 8 to 80.

0-915190-56-7 $7.95
8½ × 11   paperback, illus.

Do I Have To Go To School Today?
Squib Measures Up!

Squib dreads the daily task of going to school. In this volume, he daydreams about all the reasons he has not to go. But, in the end, Squib convinces himself to go to school because his teacher accepts him "Just as he is!"

0-915190-62-1 $7.95
8½ × 11   paperback, illus.

The Turbulent Teens
Understanding Helping Surviving

"This book should be read by every parent of a teenager in America. . . It gives a parent the information needed to understand teenagers and guide them wisely."—Dr. Fitzhugh Dodson, author of *How to Parent, How to Father,* and *How to Discipline with Love.*
0-913091-01-4 $8.95
6 × 9   paperback.

Learning The Skills of Peacemaking
An Activity Guide for Elementary-Age Children

"Global peace begins with you. Guide develops this fundamental concept in fifty lessons. If this curriculum was a required course in every elementary school in every country, we would see world peace in our children's lifetimes." — *Letty Cottin Pogrebin, Ms. Magazine*
0-915190-46-X $ 21.95
8½ × 11   paperback, illus.

Project Self-Esteem
A Parent Involvement Program for Elementary-Age Children

An innovative parent-support program that promotes children's self-worth. "Project Self Esteem is the most extensively tested and affordable drug and alcohol preventative program available."

0-935266-16-X $:3|9.95
8½ × 11   paperback, illus.

The Two Minute Lover
Announcing A New Idea In Loving Relationships

No one is foolish enough to imagine that s/he *automatically* deserves success. Yet, almost everyone thinks that they automatically deserve sudden and continuous success in marriage. Here's a book that helps make that belief a reality.
0-915190-52-4 $9.95
6 × 9   paperback, illus.

Reading, Writing and Rage

An autopsy of one profound school failure, disclosing the complex processes behind it and the secret rage that grew out of it.

Must reading for anyone working with learning disabled, functional illiterates, or juvenile delinquents.

0-915190-42-7 $12.95
5½ × 8½   paperback

A System For Caring
Supportive Counseling Techniques for Professionals and Families

Here is a book, devoted to caring and helping, that presents an orderly, simple sequence of techniques for supporting those who are hurting. Use these skills in your personal or professional life and feel enriched by the gratitude and affection of those you have helped.
0-915190-55-9 $9.95
6 × 9   paperback, illus.

Esteem Builders

You CAN improve your students' behavior and achievement through building self-esteem. Here is a book packed with classroom- proven techniques, activities, and ideas you can immediately use in your own program or at home.

Ideas, ideas, ideas, for grades K-8 and parents.

0-915190-53-2 $39.95
8½ × 11   paperback, illus.

Good Morning Class—I Love You!
Thoughts and Questions About Teaching from the Heart

A book that helps create the possibility of having schools be places where students, teachers and principals get what every human being wants and needs—LOVE!

0-915190-58-3 $6.95
5½ × 8½ paperback, illus.

I am a blade of grass
A Breakthrough in Learning and Self-Esteem

Help your students become "lifetime learners," empowered with the confidence to make a positive difference in their world (without abandoning discipline or sacrificing essential skill and content acquisition).
0-915190-54-0 $14.95
6 × 9   paperback, illus.

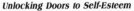

Unlocking Doors to Self-Esteem

Presents innovative ideas to make the secondary classroom a more positive learning experience—socially and emotionally—for students and teachers. Over 100 lesson plans included. Designed for easy infusion into curriculum. Gr. 7-12

0-915190-60-5 $16.95
6 × 9 paperback, illus

SAGE: *Self-Awareness Growth Experiences*

A veritable treasure trove of activities and strategies promoting positive behavior and meeting the personal/social needs of young people in grades 7-12. Organized around affective learning goals and objectives. Over 150 activities.
0-915190-61-3 $16.95
6 × 9   paperback, illus.

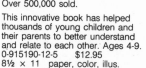

TA For Tots
(and other prinzes)

Over 500,000 sold.

This innovative book has helped thousands of young children and their parents to better understand and relate to each other. Ages 4-9.
0-915190-12-5 $12.95
8½ × 11   paper, color, illus.

TA For Tots, Vol. II

Explores new ranges of feelings and suggests solutions to problems such as feeling hurt, sad, shy, greedy, or lonely.

Ages 4-9.

0-915190-25-7 $12.95
8½ × 11   paper, color, illus.

TA for Kids
(and grown-ups too)

Over 250,000 sold.

The message of TA is presented in simple, clear terms so youngsters can apply it in their daily lives. Warm Fuzzies abound. Ages 9-13.
0-915190-09-5 $9.95
8½ × 11   paper, color, illus.

TA For Teens
(and other important people)

Over 100,000 sold.

Using the concepts of Transactional Analysis. Dr. Freed explains the ups and downs of adulthood without talking down to teens. Ages 13-18.
0-915190-03-6 $12.95
8½ × 11   paperback, illus.

Original Warm Fuzzy Tale Learn about "Warm Fuzzies" firsthand.

Over 100,000 sold.

A classic fairytale. . . with adventure, fantasy, heroes, villains and a moral. Children (and adults, too) will enjoy this beautifully illustrated book.

0-915190-08-7 $7.95
6 × 9   paper, full color, illus.

Songs of The Warm Fuzzy
"All About Your Feelings"

The album includes such songs as Hitting is Harmful, Being Scared, When I'm Angry, Warm Fuzzy Song, Why Don't Parents Say What They Mean, and I'm Not Perfect (Nobody's Perfect).
JP9003R/C $12.95
LP Record Album/Cassette

Tot Pac *(Audio-Visual Kit)*

Includes 5 filmstrips, 5 cassettes, 2 record LP album. A *Warm Fuzzy I'm OK* poster, 8 coloring posters, 10 Warm Fuzzies. 1 *TA for Tots* and 92 page *Leader's Manual*. No prior TA training necessary to use Tot Pac in the classroom! Ages 2-9.
JP9032 $150.00
Multimedia program

Kid Pac *(Audio-Visual Kit)*

Teachers, counselors, and parents of pre-teens will value this easy to use program. Each *Kid Pac* contains 13 cassettes, 13 filmstrips, 1 *TA For Kids*, and a comprehensive *Teacher's Guide*, plus 10 Warm Fuzzies. Ages 9-13.
JP9033 $195.00
Multimedia Program